TO BLESS
ALL PEOPLES

Service is the rent each of us pays for living—the very purpose of life and not something you do in your spare time or after you have reached your personal goals.

—Marian Wright Edelman
Children's Defense Fund

PEACE·AND·JUSTICE·SERIES 12

TO BLESS ALL PEOPLES

Serving with Abraham and Jesus

GERALD W. SCHLABACH

HERALD PRESS
Scottdale, Pennsylvania
Waterloo, Ontario

Library of Congress Cataloging-in-Publication Data
Schlabach, Gerald.
 To bless all peoples : serving with Abraham and Jesus /
Gerald W. Schlabach ; foreword by Michael A. King.
   p.   cm. — (Peace and justice series ; 12)
 Includes bibliographical references.
 ISBN 0-8361-3553-9 (alk. paper)
 1. Service (Theology)   I. Title.   II. Series.
BT738.4.S27   1991
253—dc20   91-15133
                                                    CIP

The paper used in this publication is recycled and meets the
minimum requirements of American National Standard for
Information Sciences—Permanence of Paper for Printed Library
Materials, ANSI Z39.48-1984.

Unless otherwise noted, the Bible text is from the *New Revised
Standard Version Bible*, copyright 1989, by the Division of
Christian Education of the National Council of the Churches of
Christ in the USA, and is used by permission.

Excerpt marked NJB is from *The New Jerusalem Bible*, copyright ©
1985 by Darton, Longman & Todd, Ltd. and Doubleday, a division
of Bantam Doubleday Dell Publishing Group, Inc. Reprinted by
permission.

TO BLESS ALL PEOPLES
Copyright © 1991 by Herald Press, Scottdale, Pa. 15683
   Published simultaneously in Canada by Herald Press,
   Waterloo, Ont. N2L 6H7. All rights reserved.
Library of Congress Catalog Number: 91-15133
International Standard Book Number: 0-8361-3553-9
Printed in the United States of America
Book design by Gwen M. Stamm/Cover photo courtesy of
   Mennonite Central Committee

1 2 3 4 5 6 7 8 9 10 97 96 95 94 93 92 91

To

Gilberto Aguirre
Verónica Argueda
José Durán
Ignacio Gutiérrez
Nicolás Largaespada

Nicaraguan Christians who walked with us and inspired my first attempts to sketch a theology of service.

Contents

Foreword

All history, and the lives of people in it, is a story God is telling. Key turning points in the story include God's promise that Abraham and his descendants would bless all people, and the coming of Jesus, who called Christians to share in blessing all peoples.

We become characters in this story and help it move forward by serving, suggests Gerald W. Schlabach. "Service," he says, "is living, being, working, and sometimes dying for others. Service is listening, crying, and standing with others."

The author identifies two extremes Christians are tempted to affirm. A faith that focuses only on God and minimizes human responsibility for the world and its suffering is not whole. A point of view that focuses entirely on human beings and minimizes God's power to inspire and direct human effort is not whole.

Schlabach effectively weaves together truths often split apart. God does initiate and empower all action in the world. Then God calls people to share and live out God's passion to bless all peoples of the world.

Schlabach's viewpoint has been shaped by his life-long commitment to the Mennonite church and its longstanding tradition of service. Despite that tradition, Mennonites have been more inclined to serve than to theologize about their service. Here Schlabach tries both to encourage service and to provide a firm biblical and theological foundation for it.

To Bless All Peoples helps all Christians better understand and worship the God who inspires service. Then it shows us ways we can serve in our situations as Abraham, Jesus, and the communities they shaped served in their settings.

—*Michael A. King*
Philadelphia, Pennsylvania

Author's Preface

During most of the last decade I have worked with Mennonite Central Committee (MCC). This agency of North American Mennonite churches is dedicated to serving as well as learning from the world's needy. In my work I have met many whose commitment to Jesus Christ and to the poor has enriched my own faith. Some have been colleagues. Some have been people I thought I would serve—who turned out to be my teachers.

My sisters and brothers face many challenges. We might expect this, for the causes of hunger, poverty, injustice, and warfare are many. But along the way I have noticed that the struggles we face as Christians tend to pull us in two opposite directions. Perhaps that is because we all long for simpler solutions.

On one hand, some long for a simple gospel that separates love of God from love of neighbor. Some Christians never really serve because of this temptation. After all, if we let the voice and the needs of our global neighbors into our heart, they may challenge us or put our faith to the test. They may even call us to the true simplicity of the gospel. This good news asks us to lay aside every comfort that might distract us from serving God and others with single-minded joy.

On the other hand, some Christians cut themselves off from the gospel that moved them toward their neighbors in the first place. The challenges that the world faces are great. Solutions are complex. So some Christians lose hope or burn out. They forget to return to the love of God they once experienced. Other Christians wonder whether commitment to Jesus Christ, his church, and his nonviolent servanthood might actually hinder effective social change.

These two challenges have shaped this book. In fact, they have shaped my view of how the church can be faithful to the calling of God. They have helped me read the Bible with fresh eyes. And this reading has shaped my theology of service.

But perhaps I should call it a theology of *servanthood*. I am convinced that God is seeking an entire people that lives and acts in servanthood. Or I might call it a theology of *mission*. We serve others in word and deed because God sends us into the world to live out the mission that God launched in Abraham.

All these terms are tied together. In Chapter 5, I will discuss the fact that many people use *service* to speak of the *deed* ministries that the church carries out, and *mission* to speak of its *word* ministries. But God calls us to do both kinds of ministry in Christlike servanthood. So using the terms this way can be confusing. Let me explain how I will be using them.

Servanthood is the way God works in the world, and

the way God calls us to live our lives. *Service* refers to our active expressions of servanthood. Love and compassion may express themselves in word or deed, but they become service when they truly seek the good of others. *Mission* refers to the fact that God calls and sends us. God calls us to something bigger than ourselves; we can be part of God's own work to create new heavens and a new earth.

Let me invite you to join me in the drama of what God is doing. Whenever we follow Christ in servanthood we will face new challenges and questions. For Jesus will lead us to the frontier between our faith and the world's need. There we will listen and linger with the people, or our labor will be of no service.

But we may also return again and again. No, we can never return to where we started on our journey before service began to change us. Yet we may always return to the biblical story for guidance. And we can always return to its central event: God has come near to humanity in Jesus Christ, who by suffering and serving became our risen Lord.

—Gerald W. Schlabach
Notre Dame, Indiana

CHAPTER 1

You Can't Keep a Good God Down

The Drama of Service

Alice wasn't sure what she had to offer to the Lord or to others. She had been giving all her life. She had brought up a family and worked alongside her husband in a small town in Michigan. But that never seemed special. It was what they had to do to make a living. Perhaps now that her husband no longer lived and she was retired, she could do more for others.

Friends suggested that she look into voluntary service opportunities offered through a church agency. She chose caring for handicapped children in Brownsville, Texas, just across the border from Mexico. Service in the name of Christ turned out not to be much different than what she had been doing all her life.

Still, Alice was in on a drama. God was drawing her, as God has drawn Christians in many times and places, into something bigger than herself. How big? As big as God's just and healing kingdom. As big as God's salvation drama. As big as heaven and earth transformed. We will find out just how big in a later chapter.

For now, all Alice knew was that the weather reports were predicting a January cold snap. She was used to the cold. But the houses of poor people in Brownsville were not prepared for the cold.

Least prepared were the refugees. Other Christian volunteers in Alice's household worked at Casa Oscar Romero, a refugee center named after martyred Salvadoran bishop Oscar Romero. The refugees, having fled warfare and economic hardship in Central America, were now in legal limbo. Until they had work permits they would have trouble providing adequate housing and winter clothing for themselves.

So suddenly Alice was serving needy people she once knew only through news reports. A friend went to a used clothing store and bought all the coats she could find. "For 24 hours we washed and mended coats every minute we could spare. It got *so* cold! The church opened its gym and people came in droves." The Red Cross got involved. Soon Alice found herself cooking beans and rice for 500 people.

"I never dreamed I would look into their faces and touch them," she said later. "Now I know 'how it is with them.' How deeply I've been affected!"

Alice thought of her own childhood in a low-income urban family. She had come full circle, returning the love and help she had received as a girl. She had been blessed by others' service. Now she knew the blessing of serving. Alice was learning that touching the world's hurts was the fullest way to be a person. "How good," she exclaimed, "to be real people in a real situation!"

Servanthood: God's Way of Being with Us

God's love has set something in motion. That something is at work in the hurting life of humanity. We may call it salvation, healing, mission, peace, justice, or the kingdom of God. And sometimes we simply pray, "Thy will be done on earth as it is in heaven."

Whatever we call God's action in the world, the only way for us to get involved is by serving. Service is living, being, working, and sometimes dying for others. Service is listening, crying, and standing with others.

Service, after all, is God's own way of being in the world. According to an ancient Christian hymn the apostle Paul wove into his letter to the Philippians (2:6-11), the earliest Christians understood the central event in their faith as service.

God's way of entering and healing the life of broken humanity was to "take the form of a slave" (or servant). And as a hurting, loving, serving person like you and me, God-in-Christ "humbled himself and became obedient to the point of death—even death on a cross."

I may best express God's love through words that encourage and invite commitment to Christ. You may best express God's love with hammer and nails, bandages and medicine, or food and drink.

Our brother may campaign to prevent homelessness, war, and hunger in the first place. Our sister may organize our gifts into a wise and coherent plan of ministry to others. But whatever each one's calling may be, we will only work with God if we work as serving, self-giving people. Then we will "give preference to others" by "pursuing not selfish interests but those of others" (Phil. 2:3-4, NJB).

But there is a problem. After we have been in the church awhile we hear words like *salvation, the kingdom of God, the Lord's Prayer*, and *service* a thousand times. It's easy to make these words little boxes and put God's plans or even God into these boxes.

But God has ways of breaking out. God has ways of loving people who hurt that may seem new, unexpected, even threatening. God loves broken humanity too much to let any box hold God back.

Service: God's Way of Breaking Out

Unlike Alice, Juan Angel thought he knew how God wanted him to serve. A few years before we met, he had begun pastoring a small church near Puerto Cortés, Honduras. A recent graduate of a Bible institute, he was full of ideas and answers.

Like many port cities, Puerto Cortés had plenty of vice. Juan Angel decided to minister to alcoholics. If some were too drunk to talk or were asleep on the sidewalk, he moved them out of the hot tropical sun.

Meanwhile, Juan Angel was just as determined to be a good pastor to a congregation in a small town outside of the city. The name of the town, *Cienaguitas*, means marsh lands. It hints at the poor living conditions of the area. If members had jobs at all they worked as farm workers or day laborers. Some of the men were fishermen. Mothers, often without husbands, worked as laundry-women or they made and sold *tortillas*. Health was poor. A common food was the crabs that feed on garbage along the beach. All the farmland in the area belonged to just three large landowners.

"I was a very conscientious pastor," Juan said. "I organized my visits systematically. I chatted, evangelized family members, and tried to encourage the flock with my enthusiasm. But as I gained the trust of the church members, and we talked about their problems, I realized their problems were economic."

Juan Angel's answers weren't answering. He knew a simple antibiotic could cure a certain sick woman. But she had no money. He believed God could cure miraculously, "But I couldn't feel right simply praying for the sick, then going my way."

What were the reasons, Juan Angel asked himself, for the unemployment, alcoholism, prostitution, malnutrition, and illiteracy? "What did God have to say about all these situations? The people wanted to know what the pastor had to say.

"Sin is the cause of all injustices. That had always been my answer, but in a general way. Now I saw that sin expresses itself in the unjust structures of society. Right around us were those landowners.

"They were living well by exploiting their employees." In Honduras, Juan Angel explained, landowners, shopkeepers, and companies often fire experienced employees so they do not have to provide retirement benefits. Then they hire others for considerably less.

Slowly Juan Angel's conviction deepened that the gospel is a total response by God to all the needs of humanity. He began describing it as an "integral" or a "holistic" gospel. He became convinced that the gospel calls Christians to work at changing the unjust structures of sin. Eventually his preaching changed.

Juan Angel had started serving his congregation in traditional ways. He had counseled, prayed, visited, preached, and evangelized. He still does all these things. But along the way, the poor people he went to serve have evangelized him, too.

"I converted twice," he said. "Or maybe my conversion to love of neighbor was my first real conversion."

To explain, Juan Angel turned to Acts 10:34-35. "It is like when Peter went to Cornelius's house expecting to evangelize him. Soon he had to confess, 'I truly understand that God shows no partiality, but in every nation anyone who fears him and does what is right is acceptable to him.' Cornelius evangelized Peter, too."

Juan Angel was right. Once Peter had neat little boxes. He thought that Jews like himself were with God in one kind of box. He thought "unclean" Gentiles like Cornelius, the Roman military officer, were in another box. God had to wake Peter with a jarring vision to get him moving.

Still, once Peter was in Cornelius's house he also had to linger. Acts 10:48 says he stayed longer than he would have before. Once God gets us moving, we must stay put long enough to learn all that God's love can mean for a community, a neighborhood, a church, a people—and for us. *God* wants to box *us* in.

Boxed in by Love

Jesus had warned Peter. Three times he asked him,

"Do you love me?" Three times a hesitant Peter answered, "Yes, I love you." Each time Jesus urged Peter to serve others, to tend and feed his sheep.

Then Jesus added, "Let me tell you something, Peter. When you were young you dressed as you wanted. You went where you chose. But you've seen more than you bargained for and you're getting older.

"I don't blame you for hesitating. In fact, I have to warn you. To tell you the truth, when you get old you will stretch out your arms and someone else will dress you—with handcuffs. Yes, they will lead you away to a prison cell. They will lead you away to death.

"So look, dear friend. You're already headed where you don't want to go. Why not let me be the one to lead you? Follow me" (John 21:15-19, paraphrased).

Throughout his life, Peter struggled and resisted as God led him. By making a commitment to Jesus and feeding his Lord's sheep, Peter had let God's love box him in. Surrounded by God's love, Peter learned new things. His Lord had sheep in other nations and cultures, people whom Peter knew nothing about (John 10:16). He learned that they had needs he knew nothing about. And he felt God stretching him to respond in new ways.

John Perkins knows how this works. Perkins was born and raised in the economically depressed and racially segregated U.S. state of Mississippi. His only way out of poverty seemed to be leaving. At seventeen, Perkins moved to California. There he married and began to improve his economic status. After finding that living only for himself and his own family left a spiritual hunger, he committed his life to Jesus Christ.

Soon Perkins was sharing his testimony throughout southern California. He preached in churches and prisons. In church circles he was becoming a celebrity. But he sensed God calling him back to Mississippi.

Today the "Voice of Calvary" ministry that Perkins founded is well-known. Many have noted its integrated approach to sharing God's love. It combines evangelism, building the church, social action, and economic development. But in 1960, when Perkins first moved back to Mississippi, he saw himself mainly as an evangelist. He would preach the gospel.

Still, Perkins always asked himself, " 'Is evangelical Christianity relevant to the black community?' Could an evangelistic faith have an impact on people who had been long-term poor?"[1]

From the beginning he and his family lived closely with their neighbors. Just as Jesus instructed his disciples to do on their first missionary endeavor (Mark 6:8; Luke 22:35), they depended on the community that hosted them for support and lived at the same level.

> As we would go out into areas like "Baptist Bottom," "Sullivan's Holler," and "Rabbit Road," as we would cut wood and farm with people and speak in the schools, we could not escape seeing firsthand the desperate physical needs of many of our people. We began to discover that real evangelism brings a person face to face with *all* the needs of a person. We had to see people not just as souls, but as whole people.[2]

Once more, God's love was setting in motion the dynamic drama of service. Perkins compares the stages in God's leading to a row of dominoes, each pushing the next one over.[3]

> First there was *the call* to live with a people. Then God had called us to share his gospel through *evangelism.* . . . He had us learn from and depend on people, so our evangelism took us into their lives. . . .
>
> Next was *social action*—trying to fill some of the needs we found and also communicate to the deep spiritual needs behind the physical demands of poverty or sickness.

At first this meant providing services like day care and health care. But Perkins quickly sensed a danger—giveaways create a welfare mentality in people. He calls these "cheap involvement designed primarily to deal with my guilt, not the problem."[4]

So he was soon moving on to "*community economic development*—because as our social action deepened, it caused us to have to deal with questions and causes behind the symptoms of poverty." Projects included leadership training, adult literacy, and economic co-operatives. These provided opportunities for employment and self-management in the black community.

"And finally, like the last domino, our witnessing and our concern and our programs led us into a confrontation with the system perpetuating many of the problems—the issue was *justice*." Perkins was learning that even day care, health programs, and co-ops brought confrontation with the racial and economic system that had long kept blacks poor.

By 1969, involvement in the civil rights movement had landed Perkins in jail. Looking back, he realized that "we were almost destined to wind up in jail. . . . We were locked in by a set of beliefs, and then to a calling that we couldn't escape if we had wanted to."[5]

He calls this being "boxed in by love."[6] It meant he couldn't leave the community. It meant a passion for making a real difference in the lives of his people. It meant expressing God's love in new ways that led to controversy and confrontation with injustice.

Where Is God Taking the Church?

We have been talking about individuals like Alice, Juan Angel, Peter, and John Perkins. Actually, God's love has led the worldwide church where many of us have not been sure we wanted it to go.

During the last two centuries, missionary efforts have spread the gospel and built new churches throughout the world at a phenomenal rate. This growth has followed the spreading culture of Europe and North America. Because of this, the Christian gospel must share the blame wherever the richness and integrity of other people's cultures have suffered.

But the gospel is having the last laugh. It is turning Christianity into a non-Western religion again! Somewhere around the year 2000 there will be more Christians in churches of the South and the East (Africa, Latin America, and Asia) than in the West.

It so happens that the peoples of the world's South and East also suffer the most hunger and poverty. The whole world strains against the imbalances our economic systems create when they take power and resources away from those who need them most. The people world suffer because a few waste resources so foolishly. Money spent on military weapons could feed and provide medical care to all children.

There are pockets of poverty and hunger everywhere. But in the nations and churches of the South and East it is harder to ignore these worldwide realities. That is because most citizens and church members there must face them every day.

Christians in these countries ask what it means to be faithful to Jesus Christ when neighbors and fellow church members die of hunger or are tortured for protesting injustice. Church leaders ask how they should relate to movements that seek change and justice.

Missionaries wonder whether they have defined their task too narrowly. Development workers sent from churches in the North and West wonder whether they should work for change back home.

So Christians are asking new and troubling questions. Yet it is not because they have abandoned the missionary task. Actually, it is because the modern missionary movement has been so successful!

A South American evangelical leader, Samuel Escobar, makes this point. Then he asks:

> Is not simple survival as human beings a right of Christians in the Third World? Shouldn't it be the concern of their [brothers and sisters] in other parts to find out what can be done? It is not only some poor individuals who pose the usual problem of charity and how to help isolated cases of human suffering. It is a whole community of believers spread out in a vast region which is fighting for its survival.[7]

Behind such questions is one people of faith have

asked throughout history. It arises whenever they confront the reality of suffering. *Does God care?*

But then another question leaps from the heart of anyone who has experienced God's love. *How can God not care?*

This is the dynamic of service, God's way of being in the world. You can't keep a good God down. You can't hold back the God who has come to us in the suffering servant Jesus.

The world's needs seem overwhelming. The questions our suffering brothers and sisters ask us are troubling. The prospect that one person, family, or congregation can make a difference looks remote.

But let's remember something: We have heard these questions and felt a bit of the world's suffering precisely because God is already catching us up into the great drama of God's dynamic love. It is the drama of God's continuous efforts to reach out, serve, die for, save, and renew humanity and all creation.

Seen in that light, we face more than a terrible problem. We face an invitation. God may call us to the most humble, down-to-earth tasks. But such tasks are part of something big, historic, and worldwide.

Questions to discuss

1. What do the experiences of Alice, Juan Angel, Peter, and John Perkins have in common?

2. Put yourself in Juan Angel's shoes. How should he carry out his ministry?

3. What new challenges and questions have you discovered through your ministry or service to others?

CHAPTER 2

And He Had Compassion

Salvation Overflows into Service

I have two children. They are among my greatest joys in life. At times they are also among my greatest frustrations. The four-year-old is especially exasperating. He is so full of life, excitement, wonder, and desire to learn. But when he is tired, his intense curiosity turns impatient. He wants to control his world, to do everything for himself—right now!

Sometimes I am ready to throw up my hands and say, "Why did I want to be a parent? I could have written this book by now. I could have *read* a book lately! Why am I taking care of this kid? Why, oh why?"

But I don't ask that question. At least not for long. And at least not very seriously.

If a parent really has to ask, "Why do I care for my child," something is wrong. If I care for a son because I want him to love me back, I am manipulating our relationship. The relationship is a little sick. Or if I care for a daughter only so she will take care of me in my old age, economics has corrupted our deep relationship.

It is fine to hope for hugs. And in many cultures of the world, children are the only social security system to provide care in old age. But in the end, these are extras. Healthy, loving parents do not care for their children because of what they get out of it. They do not need reasons. We have children in the first place because to be human is to live in relationship with others.

Serving our fellow human beings is like this. We shouldn't have to ask why we either care for, or take care of others. Even our service to God is a response to God's loving, serving person. It is not for a reason, nor for what we get out of it.

We care and serve each other simply because of who we are. We are family, one flesh, whatever our language or race. We are offspring of the same God. We share this same earthly home. We sense solidarity one with another; we "rejoice with those who rejoice, [and] weep with those who weep" (Rom. 12:15).

The biblical term for all this is *compassion*. The *com-* in compassion means sharing in *com*mon. The *-passion* is our deepest experience of life in all its joys and sufferings.

The Habit of Serving

When Jesus told the story of a person who modeled service and love of neighbor, he said little about *why* the man stopped along the side of the road to serve. Jesus simply said that he was moved with compassion.

You probably know the story, found in Luke 10:25-37. We often call it the parable of the good Samaritan, perhaps because the Samaritan's actions contrasted with those of the "good people" in society.

Robbers mugged a man on the Jerusalem-Jericho Road. He was lying half-dead when the "good people"—first a priest, then a Levite—walked on. They had "good" reasons for walking away. Holy responsibilities pressed upon them. If the man were actually dead they would be unclean and (to their way of thinking) unable to "serve."

Perhaps these good people even felt pity. But pity is not compassion. Pity condescends, or looks down on others. It need not sense a common humanity. It can remain a mere feeling. It need not act.

But along came a Samaritan. Was he actually "good"? Like all of us, he was probably a mixture of good and selfishness. But his "goodness" was not the point Jesus was making. When we call him the "good Samaritan" we risk overlooking the scandal of using him as an example. We imply that *this* Samaritan was different, as though he were a rare good one among many bad ones. That very attitude stems from suspicion, not solidarity, between different kinds of people.

The first people to hear Jesus' story would not have thought the man good at all! They would have despised him. To them, he was a mixed-breed with a mixed-up religion. The Samaritans worshiped the right God—the God of Abraham, Isaac, and Jacob—but the Jews were sure the Samaritans worshiped in the wrong way (see John 4:20).

We ought to call this the parable of the compassionate outcast. His active compassion was the point. And his social standing drove the point home. Jesus was pointing to both the possibility and the problem most of us have when it comes to serving others freely.

Almost everyone feels compassion for someone, so we know what it is. Compassion is within reach of all. But usually we feel compassion only for our own kind. Most human beings care only about their own family, tribe, church, nation, or race.

A lawyer had prompted Jesus to tell the Samaritan story. This limited caring was exactly what had kept him from serving God with all his heart, soul, strength, and mind. He claimed he wanted to keep God's law. He even knew God's intention behind the law—that we love God and love our neighbor as ourselves. But the lawyer wanted love of neighbor to stay manageable.

"And just who is my neighbor?" he asked. How far out must it extend? We can almost hear him thinking. *Surely not this group or that! Only to Jews who keep the law like I do, right? No? Then to all my fellow Hebrews, but surely not to Gentiles. And not to that disgusting mix of Jew and Gentile—the Samaritans.*

What a contrast! The Samaritan in Jesus' story did not pause to debate who his neighbor was. He did not ask whether the man qualified for humane, neighborly treatment. That is what made the Samaritan himself a neighbor to the wounded man. Seeing the victim of the highway robbery lying there stripped and half-dead, he did pause and turn away, but not from the man. Instead, he paused and turned away from his own tasks, his own agenda.

He turned *toward* the one in need, rather than walking by on the other side of the road. He did not need to ask *why* this wounded man deserved his attention, why the man's needs were more important than his own. He did not even need a sermon about service! Having compassion, he simply acted.

If the Samaritan had not acted, he would not have had compassion in the first place. But he did act. Even the lawyer eventually admitted that the Samaritan was the only one who "showed him mercy" (10:37).

Here the text in Greek literally reads, "he *did* mercy." He treated the wounds of the other, he bandaged him. He relinquished his own comfort and he set the wounded man on his donkey. He took him to an inn.

But he did not stop there. Reaching into his own pocket, he made sure the man would continue to receive care. He kept the wounded man's long-term interests in mind. And it cost him something. Most telling, he acted with no apparent expectation that the wounded man would repay him or even thank him.

Without asking the Samaritan *why* he served, we may probe deeper for the *roots* of his compassion. This was probably not the first time he had needed to travel into Judea. Here in the land of the Jews he had felt the glare of hatred and the pain of discrimination. Perhaps he needed to travel with ample provisions because he could not count on hospitality. But that made him even more of a target for the robbers. And if they beat him, it was even less likely that the Jewish residents in the region would stop and help.

As a despised Samaritan, he shared an experience of oppression with the robbery victim. He too had known vulnerability. He sensed their common humanity.

Still, oppression, hatred, and discrimination could have provoked bitterness in the Samaritan. Years of mistreatment could have made him callous. Survivors of German concentration camps in World War II say that the horrors there turned normally kind people selfish. Like trapped animals, they cared only for their own survival. Yet others who seemed just as ordinary became saints giving up their last scrap of food for others. What made the difference?

In addition to oppression and hatred, the Samaritan must have experienced some good things. Perhaps his parents were especially caring. Perhaps he had seen neighbors show hospitality even when their provisions were meager. Perhaps the story of Abraham interceding for the wicked cities of Sodom and Gomorrah had sunk deep into his heart. Perhaps a stranger's unexpected kindness had reshaped his own life forever.

Whatever its roots, the Samaritan's kindness seems to have been habitual. To live in solidarity, to sense compassion, and to act constructively in response to compassion was a deep and abiding part of him. It was part of what "made him tick." He didn't need a reason to serve, for he was a serving person.

The real question for us, then, is not why we should serve. Rather, it is this:

How do we become serving people?

How does the habit of the Samaritan emerge in our hearts and hands?

Not a "Should" but a "Therefore"

Compassion ought to flow naturally from all people. Compassion can spring from solidarity—our common human experience of being open to each other. People of every race, culture, nationality, and religion can and do show compassion. In fact, one message of the story of the Samaritan is that sometimes those we think outside the faith serve better than we do.

But would we fully recognize this if Christ had not come? After all, Jesus told this parable! Jesus showed what it means to be the human beings God created us to be. Jesus insisted that God is working to save all peoples, not just his own nation or any single nation.

Few of us would really understand solidarity if Christ had not shown God's solidarity with us. Christ entered into our human suffering. God then vindicated Jesus' nonviolent way of servanthood by raising him from death. This lets us trust that suffering service means something in a violent, selfish world. Without Jesus we wouldn't have confidence that service really can overcome injustice.

Our own compassion in response to others, then, is a response to the compassion that God has shown us by sending Jesus. Our service to others is a response to the suffering service Jesus gave us.

Without Christ's solidarity with us we might help in a soup kitchen in our spare time for the experience. We might work in another country for the adventure. But would we willingly suffer? As Paul said, "Rarely will anyone die for a righteous person—though perhaps for a good person someone might actually dare to die. But God proves his love for us in that while we still were sinners Christ died for us" (Rom. 5:7-8).

John put it this way: "We love because [God] first loved us. Those who say, 'I love God,' and hate their brothers or sisters, are liars" (1 John 4:19-20a).

Throughout the pages of the Bible, this is a pattern. To lovingly serve God and neighbor is not a *should* but a *therefore*. It is a response to God's love, compassion, and service toward us. It is a response to God's grace.

The pattern is even at the heart of God's teaching (*Torah*) through Moses. When we Christians speak of the first books of Hebrew Scripture we often call them "Law." And we (unlike our Jewish brothers and sisters) hear something harsh and negative in the word.

But for the Hebrews who first heard the *Torah* it was a word of grace. By mighty works God had made a way through the Red Sea and liberated them from cruel slavery. Now God was patiently teaching the unruly ex-slaves how to live peaceably and equitably together in the Promised Land. What a gift!

Of course the teaching of Moses does contain many laws. But obeying them did not mean obeying a harsh and fickle tribal deity. God was the one who initiated covenant with the people, saying, "I will be your God." Service would then flow as a response: "I will take you as my people"(Exod. 6:7).

How different from other religions of the day! In most it was the people who begged, bribed, and bartered just to get the attention of the gods. Serving the God of the Bible is not like that.

For the Hebrews, obeying God's laws meant treating one another as God had treated them. They had been the least of all peoples, so few and so oppressed by the Egyptians that they were barely a people. But the Lord God had loved and liberated them. God had given them a new identity as God's people. *Therefore* the only fitting response was to care for their own weak—the poor, the widows, the orphans. They could not even celebrate God's salvation at their feasts and passovers without including the weak ones! (See Exod. 22:22; Deut. 7:1ff.; 14:28-29; 16:11; 24:17-22).

But such treatment could not stop with their own kind. The Hebrews had been foreigners in Egypt. The Egyptians had discriminated against them, then enslaved them. Now they were to treat any foreigner among them fairly. They were to remember their days of slavery and free their own slaves. They were also to include foreigners in their celebrations. (See previous texts plus Lev. 25:29-42 and Deut. 15:12-15.)

Such actions were not primarily legal obligations. They were acts of thanksgiving. One of the oldest confessions of faith in the Bible appears in Deuteronomy 26. It is part of a harvest festival of thanksgiving. The Hebrews brought the first fruits of the soil to the priest and recounted,

> A wandering Aramean was my ancestor; he went down into Egypt and lived there as an alien, few in number. . . . When the Egyptians treated us harshly and afflicted us, by imposing hard labor on us, we cried to the Lord, the God of our ancestors; the Lord heard our voice and saw our affliction, our toil, and our oppression. The Lord brought us out of Egypt with a mighty

hand and an outstretched arm . . . gave us this land, a
land flowing with milk and honey. *So now I bring* the
first of the fruit of the ground that you, O Lord, have
given me. . . . I have given it to the Levites, the resi-
dent aliens, the orphans, and the widows. . ." (Deut.
26:5-13, emphasis added).

Gratitude for God's might and loving liberation
from Egypt led to a responsive and loving *therefore* (or
"so now") in which the poor in the land benefited
most. Salvation overflowed into service.

But they had to remember. Returning to the New
Testament, we find a parable that contrasts sharply
with the one about the Samaritan. It is the parable of
the ungrateful servant who forgot to remember.

A king canceled the unpayable debt of a servant,
which today would be over a million dollars. Back
then, a debt this big meant the man and his family
would be sold into slavery. Their slave labor would
then pay back at least some of the debt.

But when the man pleaded for mercy the king for-
gave him. Apparently he remained in his post. Now he
demanded repayment from a fellow servant. The sum
was only a fraction of his own debt. But he had forgotten his own debt and the king's compassion. And he
had forgotten (or like the priest and Levite, he refused
to see) what he had in common with his fellow servant.

We become serving people by gratefully remembering the love, mercy, compassion, and solidarity of
God toward us. We nurture the habit of the Samaritan
by recounting the stories of God's saving actions down
through history and in our own lives.

As we said in Chapter 1, God's love may send us out

to unexpected places, urging us to serve others in unanticipated ways. But we must also return again and again to the wellspring of our service—God's love and God's biblical story. Service must stay connected to worship among God's people. The gathering of those who respond to God's love is where we remember.

Grace Versus Good Works: Why All the Fuss?

Let's be honest, however. Prejudice toward other groups and prideful preference for our own have taught most human beings other habits, not the Samaritan's. It is also far from evident in many Christians. Lots of Christians claim to have experienced God's love. Sometimes we demonstrate the Samaritan's habit. But realistically, service does not always flow naturally from salvation, as biblically it ought. Instead, we Christians sometimes debate who the neighbor is.

You've probably heard some of the arguments. "Won't we just be trying to earn our salvation with good works?" "Isn't it their own fault that they are poor?" Or, "There is nothing wrong with social action, but won't it distract us from saving souls for eternity?"

Then there are these arguments. "Isn't it 'cheap grace' to think we can be saved by faith alone?" "Why bother working for social change through the church when it takes so long?" Or, "There is nothing wrong with relief work and soup kitchens, but won't they distract us from working to change the political system that leaves people hungry and homeless?"

Those who debate may be liberal, conservative, or (like most of us) muddling along without a label. But

our debate often shows we are more interested in justifying our own lives than giving life to others. If we
trust God to make us just, hinted Luke and Jesus, the
self that seeks self-justification is stripped of power.
We then live freely and selflessly for others!

Remember why the lawyer asked, "And who is my
neighbor?" *He wanted to justify himself.* But Jesus cut
through his pretensions (and ours!). If *you* are the
neighbor, Jesus told him, you won't need to ask. If servanthood is your way of being, you will simply serve.
*Jesus saw that when service becomes a point for debate,
the debaters may have already missed the point.*

Servanthood has everything to do with justification!
This does not mean that we serve to make ourselves
just through good works. For then we are still self-
centered and neither just nor justified. Further, our
secret selfishness mars our service to others.

Servanthood does not leave room for long debates
over whether Christians should be socially active, nor
for splitting hairs over which neighbors merit concern.
Then Jesus may wonder why we who proclaim "justification by faith alone" are *still* justifying ourselves.

Through grace, Christ has freed us from bondage to
self. This is the witness of the church. We are freed to
live for others. It should be as simple as that.

Of course it never is that simple. Sin and insecurity
still make claims on our selves. But something happens
as we continuously return, remember, and remind one
another who we are in Christ. We put on, as Paul said,
Christ's new way of being (see Eph. 4:24 and Col.
3:10ff. Cf. Gal. 3:27).

Before going to the cross, Jesus gave his disciples an

example of how to put on his new way of being. John 13 tells us that on the very night of his betrayal,

> Jesus, knowing that the Father had given all things into his hands, and that he had come from God and was going to God . . . tied a towel around himself. Then he poured water into a basin and began to wash the disciples' feet and to wipe them (John 13:3-5, 15).

Jesus could put off the divine garments of Lord and Teacher, and put on the towel of a humble servant (v. 14, cf. Phil. 2:7), because he knew who he was. He had nothing to prove, no need to justify himself. So it is with us. When we know our identity—who we are in Christ, in relation to God, and in solidarity with others—we become people freed to serve.

Questions to discuss

1. What is the difference between compassion and pity? Suggest examples of each.

2. The author makes some guesses about the roots of the Samaritan's compassion. What do *you* think motivated him?

3. What debates about service and social action have you heard? Have these debates moved people toward or away from their "neighbors"?

4. Why is it so important to remember and recount God's saving, liberating acts toward us?

5. Do you agree that there is a link between servanthood and justification? What is the link?

CHAPTER 3

In You Shall All Nations Find Blessing

Service Overflows into Salvation

Service needs more than motivation, even if that motivation is Christlike and Samaritan-like. It also needs shape and direction. So now we turn from the sources of service—compassion, solidarity, and gratitude to Christ. We turn to God's goal for service, and to God's strategy for reaching that goal. How, and with what goals do we serve when we do so "in Christ"?

Beyond the Good Samaritan

The Samaritan was one person acting for the good of one other person. This willingness to turn aside from our own concerns for the sake of "the least of these who are members of my family" (Matt. 25:40) will always be at the core of true service. Even when God calls us to more complicated ways of serving, concern for the smallest child or the weakest member of society must hold everything else together.

Perhaps the priest and Levite told themselves that to stop for this one wounded man would delay their religious work for the synagogue, or even the whole nation. But their "service" had strayed from its center.

Still, no single teaching, story, or parable can say all that God would have us learn about any matter. So it is no criticism of the Samaritan to note that his action on behalf of the roadside victim had limitations.

First, the Samaritan acted alone. God does not just call us to be lonely, heroic, Samaritans on the world's troubled highways. Thank God! When we are young and idealistic we may imagine that we, by ourselves, have to change the world. This is a recipe for burnout.

But much more is at stake. God is calling forth a people to live for all peoples. Throughout history, as we shall see, God's strategy has been to create *communities* that will live as servants of *their* communities.

Servanthood is not just an individual habit. Compassion is not just a personal virtue. When God's people are faithful to God's purpose, they organize their very life together around servanthood and compassion. Servanthood is not for a special few, but for all. It is not just for a few hours a week, but the way we shape our lifestyles. It is not for a year but for a lifetime.

Second, service is much broader than individual acts of charity. Again, thank God! God cares deeply for each creature, including "the least of these." But for that very reason, God's goal for our servanthood is much more than individual, one-by-one change.

Martin Luther King, Jr., the Afro-American preacher who led the struggle for human rights in the United States in the 1950s and 1960s, explained it this way.

> We are called to play the Good Samaritan on life's roadside; but that will only be an initial act. One day we must come to see that the whole Jericho Road must be transformed so that men and women will not be constantly beaten and robbed as they make their journey on life's highway.[1]

Do we dare dream like this? The Bible begins with a new creation and ends with a *re*newed creation. But right now, both events feel far away indeed.

What in the World Is God Doing?[2]

Our world easily discourages us. You know why. Pollution. Injustice. Sexual exploitation. Racism. Deforestation and soil erosion. National and international debt. Corrupt officials. Cynical citizens. Nuclear arms. Military dictatorships War. Torture. Terrorism. And always more mouths to feed, more sick to treat.

No wonder so few people dream of a fresh, clean creation—a creation "like new." No wonder so few really expect justice for anyone but themselves, and that only with a fight. No wonder peace is elusive and hunger rampant. And no wonder so many Christians communicate despair even when they preach "For God so loved the world. . . ."

What do I mean by that? So often the only hope

Christians offer the needy is heavenly bliss for their souls after death. If we promise hope for this life, in these bodies, the best we can offer is a tiny sphere of personal peace, or perhaps family prosperity. To the world that "God so loved" we offer only judgment and damnation. We expect the church to escape like the Ark of Noah, floating above the waters of destruction.

In other words, we have given up on God's creation! And that is a word of surrender. It is a word of despair.

But we are not the first Christians to grow discouraged. The message of Jesus was that the kingdom of God was at hand. *It was right at the door, knocking hard, even breaking in!* The picture Jesus painted was not one of ceaseless heavenly bliss for our souls. Rather, Jesus gave a word picture of a banquet table with ample food for the hungry and full human fellowship together with the Lord of the banquet (Luke 13:29, 14:15ff.). Another picture placed the disciples next to Jesus in the ongoing work of bringing justice to the nations (Luke 22:28-29).

A banquet of food means a bodily existence. Justice implies a social existence. This adds up to a new society where God's will is "done on earth as it is in heaven." Sure enough, Jesus spoke of the in-breaking kingdom as a new society. Here the favored ones would be—no, already were!—the hungry, the sorrowful, the downtrodden, the merciful, the peacemakers, the persecuted (Matt. 5:3-11, 11:2-6; Luke 6:20-26, 7:18-23).

In turn, various New Testament writers spoke of our ultimate destiny as a whole new world, "new heavens and a new earth" (2 Pet. 3:13; Rev. 3:12, 14:3, 21:1-2; see also: Isa. 65:17, 66:22; Rom. 8:19-23; Heb. 11:10,

16). Of course to those facing death they also offered this assurance: We will be with Christ until this present age gives way to the fullness of the age-to-come (Luke 16:23, 23:43; Phil. 1:23).

When Jesus did not return as quickly as the first Christians expected, however, some grew discouraged. Their hope shifted. Already by the end of the century in which Christ lived many were *only* hoping for heavenly existence for the soul after death.

By the fourth century, Christians had a growing stake in the Roman Empire. Not surprisingly, few saw God as challenging the established earthly order with a radically new one.

Now the early Christians did not think they could build God's kingdom by their own strength. Nor should we. Human projects promising to create a utopia on earth usually rely on violence and often end up in dictatorship. That is true for godless ideologies *and* for crusades in God's name. God's coming to us as a suffering servant challenges Christian efforts as well as secular efforts to forcibly usher in the kingdom!

But God's saving goal is to re-create a whole new world—not just rescue our souls from the world. That should have a profound influence on the church's ministry. In word and deed, worship and outreach, we are to speak, be, and live *good news for whole people*.

From deep within, human beings long for meaning—yes, for something that will satisfy our souls forever. But when God's healing, forgiving, and reassuring word touches our souls, we don't stop caring about this world. We still care about our food, our families, our tribes, our neighborhoods, our forests and fields and work, our music and customs and art.

As whole people we keep living in bodies, in society, on earth. In fact, if a God-given hope is deep within our souls, we will love God's world all the more. We will groan together with the Holy Spirit and with creation itself as we yearn for the fullness of salvation (Rom. 8:18-27).

Only God can bring this full salvation in the kingdom of God. Only God can complete a bridge to the future. Yet somehow it matters what we do to lay a foundation. It matters to our neighbor right away. Our best efforts to transform the Jericho road, feed our neighbor, and change the world will be partial. They will be tentative and incomplete.

But when done in Christ's name, in his servanthood character, our words and deeds will be signs of the kingdom already breaking in. They will be signs in the way that the teachings and healings of Jesus were signs.

(1) They will show what God's kingdom is like.

(2) They will call forth faith that the kingdom really can come.

(3) They will draw people to begin living in kingdom ways under the servant lordship of Jesus.

(4) They will communicate the graceful power that we all need to respond to this call.

Obviously there is a tension here. In some ways, the kingdom is *already* among us. In other ways, it has *not yet* come. To relieve the tension between the "already" and the "not yet," Christians do various things. Some are tempted to think they can force the kingdom to come through violence, or even through frenzied activism. Others are tempted to simply wait for God alone to bring the kingdom.

But if we recover the early Christian hope in a *bodily* resurrection (Rom. 8:11; 1 Cor. 15), we may do better at keeping things straight. For the new heavens and earth, where we will experience a bodily resurrection, promises to be much like Jesus' resurrected body.

In the weeks between the resurrection and the ascension of Jesus, the disciples witnessed a reality that was both like and unlike any bodily existence they knew. Jesus appeared among them when they had locked the doors in fear (John 20:19). He vanished after breaking bread (Luke 24:30-31). Obviously, this is not like our bodies. Yet Jesus was not a ghost or a hallucination either. His body was enough like it had been that the disciples could touch his wounds and serve him fish, which he ate (Luke 24:39-43).

In the same way, God's new heaven and earth will be different from anything we have known. Yet it will be easier to recognize than we may think—especially if we have imagined playing harps on clouds or blissfully floating around as spirits or angels in heaven!

According to the Hebrew prophet Isaiah, life in the new world will still involve houses and vineyards and agriculture (65:17-25). According to the authors of Hebrews and Revelation the new order will come as a city (Heb. 11:16; 12:22; Rev. 3:12; 21:2). A city *(polis* in Greek) means a social, even a political existence.

So the new world that God is bringing will be something like the resurrected body of Jesus. What then of our present service and work for social change? These are more like the resurrected body of Lazarus.

John 11 tells of the last great sign that Jesus performed before his crucifixion. He raised his friend Lazarus from the dead. Lazarus still had the same body, and surely he had to die again. Yet his very existence was such a powerful sign that the religious authorities plotted to kill him along with Jesus (John 12:10-11).

Our acts of service and the changes they bring are like this. They depend on an infusion of Jesus' servanthood power. Even so, they may pass away. Yet they are still worthwhile. They can still prolong life. And they can still point toward the fullness of God's kingdom.

But How? ³

God once grew discouraged too. At least that is the way it seems as we read the first eleven chapters of the Bible.

The biblical story began with a fresh new creation (Gen. 1-2). But humanity rebelled and, together with all creation, came under the cursed power of death (Gen. 3). The effect of humanity's broken relationship with God soon multiplied in a deadly conflict between brothers. However, God did not give up or abandon even the murderer Cain. God tempered the curse with a promise to keep death from multiplying on and on. In the children of Cain, skills to survive and even to make music multiplied. But so did the threat of violence (Gen. 4).

Humankind increased in number (Gen. 5). And in spite of God's patient oversight, wickedness also grew (Gen. 6:3, 5). If Noah had not won God's favor, accord-

ing to Genesis, God might have destroyed all crea-
tures. Instead, by saving Noah's family from the great
flood, God made a new beginning (Gen. 6-8).

Again, God tempered the curse of death with a
promise of life. The sign of the rainbow showed the
promise of God to restrain the waters forever. Genesis
9:16 leaves no doubt at all about the breadth of God's
care. This is a covenant with "every living creature of
all flesh that is on the earth."

All too soon, however, a curse again marred the relationship among brothers. This time oppressive slavery
was the result (Gen. 9:18-29). So as humanity again
grew and spread out (Gen. 10), clouds darkened the
great new beginning under the rainbow.

Sure enough, humans quickly turned God's promise
of patient care to their own ends. They wanted to
make a name for themselves, to storm heaven from a
humanly crafted tower, to enforce a false unity. But
the Lord frustrated their plans, confused their languages, and scattered them. And this time, at Babel,
God did not seem to temper judgment.

Had God given up on humans after all? God seemed
discouraged. The writers of Genesis believed all families of the earth were valuable to God. They repeated-
ly listed the genealogies of all the families they knew
(Gen. 5; 9:19; 10). But humankind had frustrated every action on its behalf. Humans had abused the gifts,
protection, and skills God gave. Providence—God's
overall activity in history—had been of little avail.

Yet God could not back out now! The Lord had
made a covenant "with every living creature." God
could not even save another family (like Noah's) with-

out working to save all of creation. Another attempt to wipe the slate of the earth clean would mean God breaking God's own covenant! The only way forward was to redeem and renew *all* the families and nations.

But how? What would work? At the close of Genesis 11 the question hung in the air. This time God offered no word for humanity that might translate the chaotic languages of Babel into a message of hope.

Yet there was a rustling in history, a sifting among the world's families. The tribes of Shem, son of Noah, now called for special attention. Among them, one clan was restless. Terah was on the move, though uncertain of his destination. But Terah had a son and a daughter-in-law, Abram and Sarai. On them our eyes focus, still wondering, still awaiting a word of hope.

The Call of Abraham

Suddenly, from out of all the families of the earth, Yahweh the Sovereign Lord chose to address one family.

> And Yahweh spoke to Abram: "Go from your land, from your kindred and from your father's house to the land which I will show you; thus I will make you a great people and bless you, and I will make your name great, so that you will effect blessing. I will bless those who bless you, but whoever despises you I will curse. So, then, all the families of the earth can gain a blessing in you."
>
> And Abram went, as Yahweh had told him; and Lot went with him (Gen. 12:1-4).[4]

The Lord's command seemed simple enough: "Go!"

For ancient people to uproot themselves and leave relatives was much harder than for modern people. But God still did not demand of Abram and Sarai nearly as much as God promised. The accent was on God's initiative. It was God who was on the move. Abram and Sarai merely had to keep up. And God would bless.

God's strategy had changed! The sphere of action was still all the families of the earth. God still longed to restore all relationships (human-to-God and human-to-human) to the potential they had at creation.

But to reach that goal God narrowed the focus of action. God called and created a distinct people. This people was to serve God by serving all other peoples. The people would not live for themselves alone! God was not calling Abram *out of the world* as God had called Noah. God was calling Abram *for the world*.

Now, to understand how God works with us and with the world, we must hold together what it means *to be blessed* and *to bless others*. The Judeo-Christian doctrine of election has been the source of much confusion—not least among the "elect"! The temptation to hoard God's blessings and to see them as a mandate for ruling over others tempts all who consider themselves God's chosen people.

Meanwhile, for many the claim that the God of the universe reveals God's self through a single family or person seems a great scandal. For them it is reason enough to reject the faith of Abraham and Jesus.

Make no mistake. Abram needed to experience the blessing of God to become a blessing. God wanted Abram to offer something new, fresh, and life-giving to all history and peoples. God achieved this by creating, through Abram, a distinct people with a new and different kind of history. This people had to know God's love and care amid all kinds of trials to offer love and compassion to suffering humanity.

Blessing meant access to land (Gen. 12:1). It meant descendants (Gen. 15; 17; 18:9f.; 21:1-7). It meant new names, a new identity from God (Gen. 12:2; 17:5; 15). Above all, it meant a covenant relationship with God. In this covenant, God's demands on Abraham were small in comparison with God's promise to Abraham.

Even so, *the blessing is never an end in itself.* Rather, it is a means to God's end. Abraham was *blessed so he could be a blessing.* Already in its first generations the Abrahamic community gave practical hints as to how.

In Genesis 18, God appeared to Abraham as three mysterious visitors. They rested and feasted and the Lord repeated the promise of a son. Sarah laughed at this, as Abraham had (Gen. 17:17). But God already was making Abraham a participant in God's purposes.

"Abraham shall become a great and mighty nation," God said. Since all peoples on earth would find blessing in Abraham, God wondered, "Shall I hide from Abraham what I am about to do" with the nation centered in Sodom and Gomorrah?

"No," God declared, "for I have chosen him, that he may charge his children and his household after him to keep the way of the Lord by doing righteousness and justice" (Gen. 18:1-19).

The "way of the Lord" meant Abraham and his family would take part in God's justice. So God even allowed Abraham to question the justice of God's own plan to destroy the two cities! "Abraham came near and said, 'Will you indeed sweep away the righteous with the wicked? . . . Far be it from you to do such a thing! . . . Shall not the Judge of all the earth do what is just?' " (Gen. 18:23-25.)

"The blessing of the nations" and the "way of the Lord" meant an earnest longing for the good of others. Abraham interceded with God's own self for the kind of justice that sought mercy, not punishment. Yes, the culture before him was corrupt. Yet as long as there was hope that some good could come from it, Abraham sought to preserve and nurture the best that remained in the wicked cities.

How different from the attitude of a descendent like Jonah. Centuries later, Jonah would gleefully await God's judgment on the wicked imperial city of Ninevah and pout when God showed mercy.

How different from the attitudes of the disciples in Luke 9:52-56. They were ready to call down fire when a foreign village hesitated to welcome Jesus!

The Abrahamic clan was too small to alter the fate Sodom and Gomorrah were bringing on themselves. But a son, a grandson, and a great-grandson of Abraham blessed other clans and nations.

In Genesis 26, Abraham's son Isaac resolved a conflict between his clansmen and the Philistines over water rights. He sealed a covenant of peace (*shalom*) with their king, Abimelech. The two groups agreed not to harm each other in any way. Then the two leaders together celebrated the Lord's blessing.

Abraham's grandson Jacob is famous for scheming against brother Esau to receive blessing. But even Jacob proved to be a blessing. His father-in-law Laban came up with his own tricks to retain Jacob's skills and his labor as a shepherd. After all, he confessed, "the Lord has blessed me because of you" (Gen. 30:27).

By the end of Genesis, an upright great-grandson of Abraham—Joseph—was in a position to preserve the lives of many during a prolonged drought (Gen. 41:57; 45:5; 50:20). Through skillful organization he saved his own clan, the powerful Egyptian empire, and neighboring nations from starvation.

Already in the first four generations of the Abrahamic community, then, models of blessing and service were emerging:

The Abrahamic people-for-other-peoples interceded with God even on behalf of cities infamous for their corruption. The community was ready to resolve conflicts peacefully so that neighboring peoples might share access to natural resources. It shared economic aid and technical knowledge. It managed resources wisely in time of scarcity, even though that meant working with the empire that would eventually turn around and oppress the descendants of Abraham.

• • •

God's purposes here are exceedingly rich. It took all of biblical history to show the wealth of meaning in God's initial word to Abraham. In fact, we are learning the purpose of God. For here, in a nutshell, is God's plan of salvation. Here, in the people-for-all-peoples, is our theology of service.

Though Jesus would later live out the fullness of

God's revelation and purposes, even his coming did not alter God's Abrahamic strategy. Rather, Jesus himself decisively fulfilled God's own way of living-for-others. In the process, Jesus created a new Abrahamic people called to live for other peoples throughout the world and throughout the ages.

Questions to discuss

1. Why are Samaritan-like attitudes needed, but not enough to insure our serving others as God intends?

2. How do you picture life in heaven? How does the Bible's promise of "new heavens and a new earth" challenge you to paint your mental picture in new ways? What difference might this make in the day-to-day life of your church or yourself?

3. Can God really change the whole world by starting with one family or small group? Could God change the world *without* starting small? Explain.

4. Do you agree that God's blessing is never an end in itself? Explain.

5. List ways that Abraham, Sarah, and their descendants were a blessing to others. Then think of a modern example to match each item on your list.

CHAPTER 4

Who Has Believed Our Report?

God Seeks a Servant People

The full meaning of God's covenant with Abraham was probably not clear to him. Abraham's descendants would struggle generation after generation, through crisis after crisis, to learn the meaning of the call that had founded their peoplehood.

It is a feat, after all, to hungrily welcome God's blessing without hoarding it. It is not easy to bless others if that means risking one's own well-being. It is hard to remember God's deliverance from slavery in Egypt without thinking God has now given us the right to dominate others. It is hard to gain our life by losing it.

Yet faithful service to God and others requires that we do these two sets of things. We must ever celebrate

God's blessing even as we give God's blessings up to others. The path of faithfulness lies between twin temptations: *dissipation* (to scatter, use up, or waste) and *exclusiveness*. The people of God must live boldly in the world without spreading themselves so thinly that they no longer have anything distinct to offer. Yet we must not maintain our distinction by barricading ourselves against the challenges, needs, and needy ones for whom God has called us together.

Times of Kings and Tests of Prophets

Land, identity, and nationhood were blessings for a nomad family. They were good news for Abraham and Sarah as well as their descendants in Egypt. Pharaoh oppressed, enslaved, and stripped them of their culture and economy. But God blessed them through liberation from Egypt. God's exodus gifts—the promised land and the Law of Moses—showed God's concern for their true interests.

But the temptation to hoard God's blessings came precisely as they acquired land and nationhood (see Deut. 8:7-20). The drama of Hebrew history and Scriptures revolves around this problem. God never let the people of God ignore it for long.

Through prophets and reformers, God asked them again and again to recall their reason for being. Would they forget that they were God's servants now that God had blessed them? Would they ignore the responsibilities that accompanied blessing?

These questions started coming to a head after the people asked God for a king. They wanted to "be like other nations," with a king who would "govern us and go out before us and fight our battles" (1 Sam. 8:20). Other nations fought and oppressed in order to secure their own self-interests at the expense of others.

Was this the "way of the Lord?" How could blessing fit such a foreign policy? And what sort of blessing would they have to offer if they were not so distinct among the nations? The covenant that had made the Lord God, their exclusive king, had made them distinct.

But now they wanted a human king, too.

In many ways the kingdom of David represented the climax and fulfillment of the good news of liberation at the Exodus. The slave people had now become a nation. They enjoyed prosperity, secure borders, far-reaching international diplomacy, and prestige.

But the balance between legitimate self-interest and servanthood—between receiving God's blessing and blessing other nations—is delicate. Blood on David's hands warned that something was wrong. Soon Solomon's efforts to secure the empire showed how much was wrong. Through diplomacy and marriages to foreign princesses, he brought idolatry right into the Jerusalem court.

Solomon's policies at home were as dangerous as his policies abroad. He subjected God's people to taxation, forced labor, and military conscription. True, he built a temple to God. For a few years the temple hid the oppression with which he built it. But Solomon's death unleashed bloodshed and political division. The spell was broken. God's people were losing life by gaining it for themselves.

The "golden age" of David and Solomon looked

brighter as each wicked and petty successor sat on the throne. But as prosperity ebbed and the dynasty ruled shrinking territory, the doubts of the people grew. A remnant of thoughtful, obedient Israelites continued to believe that God truly was Lord. But only a broader vision could explain how.

As the glory of David's dynasty faded, the original purposes of God came into sharper relief. With the nation sliding toward destruction, the prophets tried to focus the meaning of Israel's now-gloomy history.

They struggled first against the idea that God's promises of blessing were for their pleasure alone. For many Israelites it was an article of faith that God had established David's family line—not just the Abrahamic peoplehood—forever.

Such belief was popular among the ruling class in Israel. They believed that the Lord would insure the perpetual reign of David's descendants however low they sunk into corruption, idolatry, and social injustice. God had saved Israel in the nick of time before, false prophets insisted. God would do so again.

Instead, empires from the east overran Israel. They carried off the most talented children of Abraham. As the ruling class awoke from the shock of captivity, the new situation gave birth to the broadest, clearest vision of God's purpose in the Hebrew Scriptures. This vision of prophets like Isaiah later shaped Jesus' own self-identity and permeated the Christian Scriptures.

The Suffering Servant of Isaiah

In exile in Babylon, disciples of the prophet Isaiah gathered to continue praying, studying, and preserving their master's teachings. They were far from the Promised Land of their forebears. Yet they discovered that they could still practice the faith of Abraham, Sarah, and Moses. God heard their prayers even here.

Truly God was Lord of all the earth. The exiles still longed to return to their homeland. But they could do good even in the city of their captors. So insisted a fellow prophet, as he urged the exiles to settle down and seek the welfare (the *shalom*) of the society in which they now found themselves (Jer. 29:4ff.).

What did this all mean? From various sources, songs emerged about a "Servant of the Lord" who would finally be faithful to God's purposes even through suffering. The example of Isaiah himself inspired his disciples. He had suffered much yet persisted when the nation rejected his warnings.

The exiles were surprised to discover they could serve the Lord even as captive civil servants of a Gentile emperor. And their longing for a new exodus back to Jerusalem opened them to renewed hope—a Messiah who would liberate God's people once and for all.

The "Songs of the Servant" appear in Isaiah 42:1-9; 49:1-6, 50:4-11; 52:13—53:12.[1] Sometimes these songs seem to refer to a dynamic prophet among the exiled disciples of Isaiah. Sometimes it seems that a remnant of Israel itself would become the Servant by learning the lessons of captivity and faithfully adhering to the just ways of the Lord (see Isa. 41:8-10 and 51:1-2). And sometimes the songs hint at an altogether faithful Servant-Messiah still to come.

Since God had called *all* Abraham's children to be a blessing, all these meanings may apply. The whole people was to be the Lord's Servant. But if Israel failed, a single Servant, faithful despite suffering, might take their place. He would serve all peoples as the people of God were meant to. At the same time, he would form a new people-for-other-peoples.

From the first "Here is my servant" onward, the Songs of the Servant bear a twin focus that is faithful to the call of Abraham. The Spirit of God would anoint the Servant to free the Israelite exiles, open their eyes to God's continuing care for them, and lead them home in a new exodus.

This meant renewed blessing for the children of Abraham. But the Servant "will not grow faint or be crushed until he has established justice in the earth." Even the farthest "coastlands wait for his teaching." The Servant would bless all peoples (Isa. 42:1-9)!

So God's love was inclusive. The Servant's mission would be global. All the nations were to gather together to hear the witness of the Servant (43:8-13). In fact, "It is too light a thing that you should be my servant to raise up the tribes of Jacob and restore the survivors of Israel; I will give you as a light to the nations, that my salvation may reach to the end of the earth" (49:1-6).

The Servant would establish justice, witness, and give light, but at great cost. The Servant would be despised. His own people would reject him (49:7, 53:2-3). The nations would misunderstand him (52:15).

And this was only the beginning. The Servant faced blows, insults, spitting, and death. Yet he did not rebel against God's way of working justice and liberation through servanthood. Rather, he trusted that God would vindicate him (49:7; 50:4-7; 53:4-10). Ultimate-

ly the Servant would prosper, "be exalted and lifted up
. . . very high (52:13).

This way of achieving justice and liberation for the
nations is difficult for all people in all times to understand, including us. What is clear is that this Servant is
one who lives and dies for others. He lives and dies for
the very nations who are astonished at his ugliness and
offended at his apparent weakness (52:14-15)!

In response, the kings of the nations are startled and
tight-lipped. Dimly they perceive what they never expected to see. The way of suffering service, not domination, is most powerful. In spite of their rejection, the
Servant bears their sufferings and sorrows, their guilt
and wounds. The Servant reconciles them, in spite of
their rebellion. This Suffering One, living and dying
for others, makes many just (53:4-11).

Along this path to justice and liberation of *all* nations the Servant would restore the Abrahamic people
to their own role as Servant of the Lord. The songs and
prophecies of the disciples of Isaiah gave many exiles
courage to return to their homeland.

But after exile, the community of Israel did not
quite know what to do with the larger vision of the Suffering Servant. What nation can be restored to prosperity yet remain a suffering servant of other nations?

In centuries following the return from exile, new
questions arose. Did they need a state and a sovereign
territory to be a people? The Maccabbeans and Zeal-
ots who revolted against foreign domination of Pales-
tine insisted that God's people needed their own state.
But new Jewish communities dispersed through the
Mediterranean (the "Diaspora") showed they could

remain a distinct people even amid other peoples.

And was there not a danger of mixing too freely with other races and cultures? Ezra and Nehemiah insisted on strict separation and refused to tolerate any inter-marriage. But the writer of Jonah called for greater, more loving openness. After all, even "Ninevah" and other centers of political power Israelites resented, might repent.

Too often in their history, the blessings of land and nationhood had tempted God's people to exclude oth-ers from God's purposes. Too often they had walled themselves within a narrow nationalism. They could never be a blessing to other nations that way.

Yet to lose the distinct identity of God's blessing through Abraham was no answer, either. There is a story that ten tribes were lost during the Exile. Per-haps it is a legend. But it reminds us that the people of God could not be a blessing if they simply fell apart.

They did not dare cease to "Hear, O Israel!" They had to keep loving the Lord with all their hearts, to carry God's Torah on their hearts, to teach it diligently to their children, to speak of it always (Deut. 6:4ff.). If they ceased, they would be finished as a people.

Only a lively, creative tension can avoid both exclu-sion and dissipation. As the American theologian Reinhold Niebuhr once showed, individuals may sometimes love others, but social groups are by nature self-interested.[2]

One message of Isaiah is this. When the people of God were shaped by the story of Abraham, relied on the power of God, were anointed by God's Spirit, they just might break the chains of collective self-interest.

But after so many centuries could anyone really expect a converted, self-giving peoplehood to emerge?

At best, imperfectly. And only if God entered human history directly. Only if God sent the suffering, self-giving Servant.

Jesus, the One-for-Others

In Chapter 2 we studied the compassion of the good Samaritan. We suggested that by remembering God's compassionate acts toward us we develop compassion and neighborliness.

The same holds true for the servant peoplehood that God has been forming throughout history. Ultimately, a people-for-other-peoples could only emerge because God became the person-for-others. We love because God first loved us. We are servants because God sent the Servant.

In the second and third centuries of the Christian era church leaders interpreted the parable of the good Samaritan in an allegorical way. (In other words they thought that each part of the story had a hidden, symbolic meaning). The thieves represented sin and the devil; humanity was the roadside victim.

When the law and the prophets failed to rescue humanity, they said, Christ came along. He cared for us, began to heal us, and with his own life paid the downpayment that would restore us to life. So the good Samaritan was really Christ.

For many years I rejected this interpretation entirely. Making the parable into an allegory seemed to blunt its harsh but obvious message. The allegory hid the fact that the church too could become as complacent toward the needy as the priest and Levite were. Perhaps this interpretation even led to complacency.

I still believe that we must keep Jesus' message about love of neighbor central as we interpret the story. But I've begun to admit that those ancient church leaders had a helpful insight. It is because Jesus became the compassionate outcast for us that we can follow the way of the Samaritan for others.

Just as the Samaritan cared for, foresaw, and provided everything the roadside victim needed to recover wholeness, Jesus sought to make humanity whole in every way. His life work, climaxing on the cross, brings forgiveness before God, reconciliation between people, and liberation from the unjust structures of our world. His resurrection and outpouring of the Holy Spirit empowers us to live the life together that God intended for humanity.

Because Jesus became the Servant whom the Lord had been seeking since Abraham, God's people can finally become a servanthood people. Because Jesus was the person-for-others, we can be a people-for-other-peoples.

When Jesus inaugurated his ministry in his home synagogue in Nazareth he read from Isaiah. God's Spirit was upon him, he said, to bring good news to the poor, proclaim release for prisoners, give sight to the blind, to free the oppressed, and announce a new beginning of justice and economic redistribution. The project that Jesus announced was so radical he nearly got himself stoned (Luke 4:16-30).

But actually, Jesus' claim to be the Servant of the Lord was not what provoked his fellow citizens. They were glad to welcome God's blessings. But they wanted them only for themselves. So Jesus reminded them that God often chose to work through and to bless people of other nations. *That* is when a lynch mob formed.

Had Jesus chosen to be a messiah who saved and served Israel at the expense of other peoples, he might never have been executed. He rejected the main political options of his day—not because they were political, but because they were all nationalistic. Jesus made the entire Servant vision of Isaiah his own, including its international, intercultural scope.

Re-creating Abraham's People-for-All-Peoples

The first Christians immediately recognized and proclaimed Jesus as the Servant of the Lord whom Isaiah had described (see Acts 3:13-26; 4:27-30; 8:26-35).

In an early hymn, which Paul quoted in Philippians 2:6-11, they expressed their conviction that servanthood was at the heart of who Jesus was. To become like human beings in every way, Jesus had given up "equality with God . . . emptied himself," and taken "the form of a slave" (or servant).

But the identity of Jesus also had immediate consequences for the new community of disciples who followed him. The "mind of Christ" that motivated his servanthood was to be their own. Jesus had insisted that a servant is never greater than the master (John 13:16; 15:20).

As Jesus washed the feet of other people, so might they. As he suffered and died, so might they. To achieve God's purposes, they too should use power different from the world's (Mark 10:41-45).

Servanthood, then, was not a command. It was not an option. It was not for a specially-called few. It was not an extra "way of perfection" for a few Christians particularly serious about faith. All believers were to be servants from the moment they began life "in Christ" (see Gal. 3:27; Eph. 4:23-24; Col. 3:9b-15).

As these servant-believers formed a community that embodied Christ for the world, it had to be international and intercultural. Putting on Christ's "new person" did not simply mean that individual believers took on a new Christlike character. Rather, it meant forming a new collective entity where old barriers of race, class, and gender broke down (Gal. 3:28; Eph. 2:13-18; Col. 3:11).

The early church still needed to work out much about how to be a servant people, a blessing to all nations. The book of Acts and the letters of Paul reveal a church struggling with many practical and theological issues as Jew and Gentile began relating in one body. Hebrew Christians had reason to fear dissipation. Gentile Christians had reason to feel excluded as second-class citizens.

The apostle Paul strove mightily to lay out a path between dissipation and exclusion. We know him as the apostle to the Gentiles. We read in Acts and Galatians how he boldly defended the right of Gentile churches to welcome and apply the gospel in ways appropriate to their own cultures. Paul wanted to spread the gospel widely, to take its blessing to all nations.

But Paul also worked vigorously to keep the gospel

from mixing uncritically with Gentile ways. To him, the church was a "new Israel." With its distinct identity and lifestyle it was to be just as "transformed" and "nonconformed," as those who received the teaching of Moses at Sinai were to be holy and set apart among the nations (Rom. 12:1-2).

The letters of Paul show many efforts to deal with problems that the disorderly, once-lawless Gentiles had in living the Christian life (Eph. 2:1-3, 11-12). The Jesus story dare not become one more "mystery religion" current in the Mediterranean world. Rather, it was to change that world (Acts 17:6).

The very existence of a reconciled, servanthood community in the midst of the nations was a service. It defied the wisdom of all the world's ruling powers. God had a different wisdom! If bitter enemies like Jew and Gentile could live for each other, what else might start to change? In Christ and through the church, God was working "to reconcile to himself all things, whether on earth or in heaven, by making peace through the blood of his cross" (Eph. 1:15—2:22; Col. 1:15-29).

A community where rich and poor, Jew and Gentile, simple and cultured all loved each other and served others challenged the current order. It set an example that many in power found dangerous. Its very existence publicly showed that the injustice, violence, and prejudice of the current order were false, failed, and fading. These were not the inevitable fate of humanity after all. They were not and are not "just the way things are" (Col. 2:15).

Violent domination is the very opposite of ser-

vanthood. Many believe it is necessary to hold together a social order. But no, affirmed Paul, it is Christ who
holds all things together—the very Jesus whom the so-
called powerful had crucified! Together with his
church, Jesus had begun transforming the present order of things (Eph. 1:19-23; Col. 1:17-18).

Though cosmic in scope (Rom. 8), Christ's great
transforming work always begins with simple, almost
mundane acts of hospitality, encouragement, mercy,
and blessing (Rom. 12). And not just to fellow Christians. "Give the same consideration to all others alike,"
urged Paul. "Pay no regard to social standing, but meet
humble people on their own terms. . . . As much as
possible, and to the utmost of your ability, be at peace
with everyone" (Rom. 12:16-18, NJB).

"God's holy people" are not the exclusive object of
Christian servanthood. Even persecutors are to bene-
fit. When God's people are faithful they simply cannot
keep God's blessing to themselves.

Questions to discuss

1. How are Christian groups tempted to become
"exclusive"? How are they tempted to "dissipate"?
Give some examples of each.

2. God called the children of Abraham and Sarah
both to receive and to be a blessing. What did this
mean for Isaiah and other prophets? For Jesus? For
the early Christians? What does it mean for you?

3. Can individual Christians serve their neighbors as
God intended unless they are part of a Christian community that as a group is also a servant?

CHAPTER 5
Doing unto Others

When Service Is a Problem

The Abrahamic community is our model of service. In such a community there is something innovative, something to celebrate, something of God's love. But that something opens out to all other communities and peoples. Otherwise the Abrahamic community has lost its reason for being. God blesses it to make it a blessing. God gives it the gift of peoplehood—for the sake of other peoples.

We have carefully traced the biblical story of God's attempt to create Abrahamic communities. It is a vivid story, with all the twists and turns of any drama. But it is more than that. For it will shape our own stories if we let it shape how we look at our lives, congregations, and communities. And it will provide a framework for the practical problems we face as soon as we roll up our sleeves and begin the work of serving.

The way of life to which God called Abraham, Sarah, and their descendants is at the heart of Jesus' teaching. At first, that may not be obvious. But everything Jesus taught about love confirms it. To love others indiscriminately, according to Jesus, is God's way.

God "sends rain on the righteous and on the unrighteous" alike. Jesus taught that to take on the character of our heavenly Parent we must love like God. God loves without excluding anyone. So we must love enemy as well as neighbor. And if we are to love enemies and neighbors alike, then surely we are to love everyone in between. Whether or not they are Christians, or join our churches, our lives of service are available to them (Matt. 5:43-47).

Anything less is simply to continue living in our old, tired, uninspired ways. Even tax collectors "love" those in their own group. Today we might say even drinking buddies take care of their own. If Christian service only means "taking care of our own kind" in the church, it will fall short (Matt. 5:46-48).

It is true that Paul taught us to "work for the good of all, *and especially for those of the family of faith*" (Gal. 6:10, italics added). But that is because the Abrahamic community must show, by its example, that the changes it proposes for society do work.

Besides, mutual aid (service in a given community) can create habits and sharpen skills that soon become available to others. Such spill-over is the least we can expect of a community that takes love of neighbor seriously. After all, the second greatest commandment teaches you to love others "as yourself" (Matt. 22:39; Mark 12:31-33; Luke 10:27; Gal. 5:14; James 2:8).

As yourself applies to the church as well as the individual Christian. An Abrahamic community values, preserves, and serves other communities "as itself." It celebrates the good in other social groups as much as its own blessings from God. Any proclamation of the gospel or any work of service that destroys what is life-giving and healthy in other communities betrays its own source—God's love.

The golden rule has taught this all along. "In everything do to others as you would have them do to you," Jesus said (Matt. 7:12; Luke 6:31). Many people know these words as a lofty ideal—easier to quote than practice. But as a concise guide for the social relations of the Abrahamic community, it is surprisingly practical.

When Things Fall Apart

God has chosen to work through people, not angels. To be sure, God's favored strategy is to work through a servanthood people. But its members are no less human than those whom they serve or join in service.

It should not surprise us, then, that Christ's way of servanthood often gets mixed up with other ways of trying to help people. These ways of helping may resemble Christlike service but actually serve other interests. Paternalism, imperialism, and triumphalism are three examples. We will define them later.

Certain kinds of evangelism and missionary work belong on this list, too. So does philanthropy, benevolent work, and "charity." As surely as Christ works to transform the world, Christ's own servanthood must change our attempts to serve.

Things Fall Apart, a novel by the African writer Chinua Achebe, tells how tribal village life came unraveled when white men arrived.[1] The main character is an elder and warrior named Okonkwo. His own mean and hard-driving spirit was part of his undoing. Injustice and deep social divisions already plagued the traditional culture. But in the end, efforts to help from the outside did as much damage as good.

Midway through the story, the first white missionary appeared. Okonkwo's son Nwoye was as sensitive to suffering as his father was violent. He did not understand the new religion. But its poetry touched his marrow and haunted his young soul.[2]

To his father's dismay, Nwoye eventually joined the little church at the edge of the village. So did many of the least valued village members—even the outcasts. Novelist Achebe recognized that the gospel can mean dignity and good news to the poor.

But from the beginning the white missionary brought more than the gospel. News that white men had brought a new government arrived even before he did. It was rumored that white men had massacred another village after its leaders killed a missionary. So the service of the gospel came mixed with colonialism. The power of a European empire backed both.

In the first sermon in Okonkwo's village, the missionary also offered consumer items. The villagers had heard of bicycles, which they called iron horses. The missionary promised to bring many iron horses.[3] Sure enough, in a few years white men built a trading store and paid great prices for products that the villagers had once taken for granted. Today we would call it economic development. But when is it a service and when is it an omen?

The missionary did try to learn about the religion of the clan. The clan's elders told him they already believed in a single High God who had created the world. They considered it a sign of respect for this distant God when they asked ancestors and lesser gods to intercede on their behalf.

The missionary concluded that village leaders would not respond to direct efforts to convert them. He tried another approach: a school and a small hospital. Soon the "white man's medicine" was turning villagers into court messengers and clerks in the white man's government.[4] Prestige grew for alumni and missionaries alike. So did churches.

But service had become a hook for evangelism. Was it still service? Was this kind of evangelism really good news? Not only the old village ways, but the initial service of the gospel message seemed to be falling apart.

Maybe some things do need to fall apart for healthy social changes to take their place. The religion and customs of the clan held many in fear. They excluded others—the outcasts—entirely.

But many customs also held the clan together. For example, there were long-established customs for settling land disputes. Okonkwo rightly wondered how the white man could decide such cases without understanding their customs or even their language.

Still, Okonkwo's fellow elders seemed simply resigned to their fate. The clan was divided. The white man had won over many of the villagers. Whites were a knife severing the ties binding villagers together.[5]

In the end Okonkwo's rage led him to vengeance and suicide. The reader is not surprised, for the novelist has been honest about his violent streak. Besides, the fatalism of fellow elders and the power of foreign colonialists had closed off constructive ways for the clan to maintain unity amidst change.

Yet a question lingers. Do so *many* things have to fall apart?

Sorting Out Mixed-up Service

Although Chinau Achebe's novel is fiction, it portrays fairly the way Christlike service can get mixed up with other kinds of power, attitudes, and interests. It also shows how even well-meaning efforts to help can bring mixed results.

In its 1987 *State of the World* report, the Worldwatch Institute warned that "our relationship with the earth and its natural systems is changing, often in ways we do not understand. . . ."

Economic progress may temporarily improve our lives. But it may also deplete resources and poison the environment for new generations. Humanity is caught in a bind. "Efforts to improve living standards are themselves beginning to threaten the health of the global economy." We must redefine progress, warns Worldwatch—soon.[6]

Many people who have gone to another country to serve in Christlike ways will recognize questions like Achebe raises and dilemmas like Worldwatch notes. Even those who try to serve the needy in their own country often discover that new and unexpected problems result from well-meaning efforts.

Those who receive may lose the incentive to help themselves. Would-be community leaders may use new training to escape poverty. They may fail to serve their neighbors so the community can overcome poverty together. An ethnic neighborhood that has suffered together, but has been united, may now find that it, too, can "no longer act as one."

Wait a minute. Part of the problem is that we tend to define service only as "helping." Worse still, we define helping as a one-way street.

This is *paternalism*. It arises when would-be servants treat others condescendingly, like parents toward children. We claim to know all the solutions. We act like the only ones who can solve problems. So we "solve" problems by doing *for* rather than *with* others. In the process we usually create new problems.

Imperialism is the form paternalism most often takes in the secular realm. It happens when one group not only believes it has the solutions, but uses its political, cultural, military, or economic power to force these solutions on others. The group may say—or even believe—that it aims to help others. But its real motive is to build its own empire, whether small or large.

Triumphalism is the form paternalism often takes in the religious realm. It arises when a church is so sure its cause will triumph that it acts like it alone possesses truth. It may only wield the power of persuasion—which is fine. But it tries to change others without allowing others to change them in any way.

Especially dangerous is the triumphalistic church

supported by secular, imperial power. That is what happened in the colonial era. It still happens whenever Christians mix up their service with the cause of their favorite political or economic system.

Another Look at the Golden Rule

A simplistic reading of the golden rule can actually contribute to paternalistic forms of service. When I am hungry, I want food from the refrigerator. So that must be what you want. I'll give you food; that will solve your problem. What about tomorrow? Oh yes, I forgot the refrigerator. No electricity? Don't worry. I know an agency that can put it in for you.

Okay, that was *too* simplistic. Obviously it takes a lot more than a refrigerator full of food to feed a hungry family. In a week the family will use up the food. In a month or a year or a decade the donor will leave. In the meantime, many other families may be going hungry.

But the refrigerator is a symbol of how different another culture or food system can be. Outsiders who want to help must learn to do differently if they want to "do unto others" as Jesus intended.

Many people in the world find more security in a small plot of land than in a refrigerator. The jobs they need to buy and stock the refrigerator may come and go. But the land will stay. What if drought comes? They turn to family and neighbors. That is why clans or villages must stick together. Traditional societies have invisible networks of sharing that help the most vulnerable members survive hard times.

Markets, soil, water supplies, and rain forests are

also part of any food system. But the wrong kind of aid may lower local food prices and put farmers out of business. Imported fertilizer may increase production for awhile but poison the village well. Large-scale development projects may damage the ecological balance, alter weather patterns, and cause erosion.

This may not be obvious to the outsider at first. True, she may have valuable skills and ideas to offer. New agriculture practices may actually improve the soil and stop erosion. Landless farmers may need legal aid, moral support, political backing, or organizing skills to acquire it. But she must work alongside community members. She must serve by listening before serving by helping. Otherwise she may disrupt unseen webs.

In any case, there are many other simplistic ways of reading the golden rule. I like blue jeans and jazz and cheeseburgers—so I assume my culture will be good for you and your kids. I value personal freedom to live where and how I want—so I assume my country's form of democracy is the best for you.

I worship God in one way—so I assume my way is the best way for you to worship God. But if my people, culture, and I destroy your community's identity, culture, or cohesion, I will have done you a great *dis*service in the name of service.

Our doing unto others can do better than this. Humans do not live by bread alone. They live also by solidarity, social connections, cultural rules. Development workers soon learn that no lasting solutions are possible without community organization and cooperation. Christlike love moves us to feed the hungry, but it should move us to nurture these as well.

Do we mean it when we say we want to do unto others as we would have them do to us? Then we must live as servants of these values of others.

The practicality of the golden rule comes into play when we turn it into a question—again and again. Would we really like someone to solve all our problems for us? Would I like it if they ignored my ideas? How much could I accomplish without a sense of self-worth? What kinds of community support would I need if I were to risk changing the way I produce or cultivate or raise my children? What resources are already present in the community for solving problems? Who are the wise elders who remember how people used to till the land or resolve disputes?

Is there anything in what we are proposing that will undermine relationships within the community? Anything that might undermine the community's relationship to the natural creation? Could we answer these questions in our own society, and if not, should others trust our advice?

If we do not know the answers then we had better ask! If we do not know people well enough to receive frank answers, then we had better live closely enough with them to earn their trust. And if our hosts do not know all the answers either, then we had better linger and work together long enough for a common wisdom to emerge.

We now discover that we too are the needy. If nothing else, we need the wisdom of others to be of service to them. More likely, we also need the service of their examples, faith, and hospitality to work at the problems in our own culture and clean up our own messes.

Meanwhile, we have discovered one thing that is sure: we need each other. We are interdependent. True service is mutual. It is a two-way street. Only as we empower one another will we serve in Christlike ways. Real change requires the participation of all. Top-down solutions will at best create new problems. There is no place for paternalism. It just won't help.

Word and Deed: One in Servanthood

Precisely because the Christian church values its own community, it must value the community of others. Just as the Abrahamic community celebrates the blessing of God that has given it life, it treasures the good that gives life to other peoples. As the children of Abraham serve, this is their golden rule.

But what about the religions of other peoples? If we are serious about our Christian faith it gives meaning and structure to our lives. We may not welcome attempts by other people to convert us to their faith. Likewise, others may not welcome our converting them.

If we live in the pluralistic modern societies of North America and Europe, such attempts may merely be a nuisance. We are used to a "marketplace of ideas." But in more traditional cultures, religious beliefs are often the glue that holds the community together. Serving a community may seem to conflict with proclaiming a belief system that might undermine community in its current form.

Do we apply the golden rule here too? Does treating others as we want to be treated mean not sharing Jesus Christ? The question often presents itself as the problem of how to "integrate word and deed."

Some Christians emphasize the need to communicate Jesus Christ in word. Their gift is to introduce others to Christ, explaining who he is in languages and images that others understand best. They then guide new believers in the first steps of the Christian life, assembling them in new congregations or welcoming them into established ones. We often call these activities evangelism, church planting—or simply *mission*.

Other Christians emphasize communicating Jesus Christ in deed. Their gift is to express the love of God in actions that heal the world's wounds and demonstrate Christ's character. They right injustices, empower the poor, and make peace in situations of conflict. We often call these activities relief, development, advocacy, diaconal ministry—or simply *service*.

Christians dedicated to "mission" sometimes worry about their colleagues in service ministries. They ask when development workers will get around to urging people with whom they work to trust in Christ. They fear that social activists downplay the spiritual roots of social problems. They stress that Jesus is the only answer to humanity's problems.

Meanwhile, Christians dedicated to "service" worry about their missionary colleagues. They warn that if we mix evangelism and social projects we may attach strings to the love service expresses. They complain that planting churches often divides communities and blocks their organizing process. They stress that God is present and active in all of human history.

So word and deed do not always seem to be one. Instead, they sometimes seem in tension. That may be okay.

Remember what we said in the last chapter? "The path of faithfulness lies between twin temptations: *dissipation* and *exclusiveness*." Christlike servants long to see new clusters of Christian disciples form *and* to see all present communities and cultures brought to their fullness.

Christians who feel the tension will be servants, whatever their primary gifts and ministries may be. If they work in what we usually call "mission," they will do so with deep reverence for their host communities. They will be excited at the chance to meet Christ in new ways. The missionary in *Things Fall Apart* missed such a chance. In Jesus the distant High God of whom the elders spoke was coming near the clan. But they could not recognize Christ this way if he did not.

Meanwhile, Christians in "service" activities will know that their most important investment is in a core group which will continue to serve after they themselves leave. This core group is the Abrahamic minority within the larger community. It is the key to continuing change. The key to its durability is a center of faith and biblical reflection.

If we are sensitive to local needs then we will allow God to create community in new and surprising ways. A group may look like a church. Or it may look like a community organization. But whatever form it takes, it will both be more healthy as a group and more effective within society if it is "Abrahamic" in character. In other words, if it has both a strong spiritual center and an outward-looking concern.

We should still hope to reveal Christ as the fullest expression of God. For we trust that his life holds all things together (Col. 1:17). We believe that his way is the only way to fully know God's life (John 14:6). But we only reveal Christ when we truly seek the good of others. God knows we reveal little of Christ when we believe our culture or religion is superior.

Problems with both "word" and "deed" ministries arise when we seek to do them in some other way—and with some other power—than Christlike servanthood. The best mission happens when the missionary seeks to discover Christ anew in her host culture. The best service happens when the community organizer, social activist, or development worker helps people to find their own solutions.

Dig down deeply enough into either form of servanthood and you will find that they meet at their core.

Questions to discuss

1. Define in your own words what it means to be an "Abrahamic community." Suggest possible examples.

2. Compare Matthew 5:46-47 and Galatians 6:10. Do you see a contradiction here? Explain.

3. Have you seen Christlike service get mixed up with other ways of "helping"? Give examples. Are any of your examples cases of "paternalism," "cultural imperialism," or "religious triumphalism"? (See page 75, or turn to the glossary at the end of the book.)

4. Does it change your understanding of service to think of it as a two-way street—giving *and* receiving, helping *and* learning? Explain.

5. How do you think Christians should "integrate word and deed"?

CHAPTER 6

Abrahamic Minorities Unite!

Models for Service Today

God began something in Abraham. The church takes part in it through Jesus. And others sometimes take part in it whether they realize it or not.

What is it? God's way of working for change. It is change that starts with us (whoever we are). It is living in communities of service to others, not just ourselves. It is a community that models the changes it works for in the world.

Look around you. Wherever good things happen in the world you will find a cluster of people somewhere in the middle. They are committed. They hope. They act. And they inspire hope in others. Like Abraham, they have believed that change could come, despite all appearances. And they are acting on their belief, without waiting around for everyone else.

At first these groups are small minorities. But they do not become discouraged when opposed. By taking an initiative, even at personal cost, they show that the changes they propose are possible. Their example inspires more and more people.

Look around. In eastern Europe, tiny bands of dissidents hammered away for human rights, until communism crumbled. In Latin America and parts of Asia, grassroots Christian communities have shown that the poor can recover their dignity and work for justice. In North America, when the government ignores the homeless, the hungry, the abused, or the environment itself, voluntary organizations arise to work for change.

A former Roman Catholic bishop in Brazil, Dom Hélder Câmara, has helped me see how important such groups can be for nonviolent social change. As Dom Hélder once said, "In the womb of all races, of all religions, in all countries, in all human groups," are change agents whom the Spirit of God is raising up.

Often, "they already exist, we do not need to create them." These groups Dom Hélder called "Abrahamic minorities," for "like Abraham, they hope against hope and decide to work, even to sacrifice, for a world more just and human."[1]

"Abrahamic minorities unite!" Dom Hélder often preached. Maintain your identities, your name, and even the distinct sources of your hope, he urged. But form a broad alliance as you work at local problems and local injustices while developing a global perspective. (1) Start where we are. (2) Learn about the global dimensions of local issues. (3) Then weave networks of common concern.[2]

Of course, not every cause is as worthy as it looks at first. When we Christians work with other people and groups, we will find both common and conflicting values. At times God will call us to criticize like prophets. At times God will call us to encourage like shepherds. Both actions can be a service. We will need help from the Holy Spirit to discern what is needed when.

Yet if we are to be the people of Abraham and Sarah, this is the way. Christ has given us a life that we only gain by losing. Our identity as a people-for-all-peoples is one that we lose as soon as we keep it to ourselves. The golden rule invites us to welcome the initiatives that other "Abrahamic minorities" take.

So without valuing our identity in Christ any less, let us join with other people of good will who truly seek to serve their neighbors. Remember: the good Samaritan was just that kind of person.

Getting Started: Three Questions and Three Stories

The Abrahamic model of social change has a practical advantage. You can always begin where you are. The two most important resources for service are already available to your congregation or home Bible study—the Spirit of Christ, and one another. Later, finances and material goods may help (or may not!). You may need information, but finding it depends mainly on your own persistence. So these resources are not the key. Organizing together in hope is the key.

Since we can always start where we are, I have not needed to search far for encouraging stories of service.

The first comes from a congregation where I was once a member. The second is from a close family friend. Although the third is from a country I have never visited, it involves an organization I have worked with.

Where Do We Begin?

The East Goshen Mennonite Church has enjoyed rich fellowship. It has also suffered the pain of division. The congregation began as an outreach to a low-income part of town. Only a few members live in the neighborhood. Most drive to church from outside.

Differing visions of how to serve in the neighborhood brought tension and conflict. Efforts to agree on a congregational program got mired in committees. Business meetings ended in resentment.

Lately the church has taken a different approach. Copastor David Miller explained it to me. If anyone feels called to respond to a need, he or she stands up and tells about it. Then, if others share the same concern and want to form a group, the church considers that a decision. Service is now out of committee. It is in the hands of those who take ownership.

If the new group meets a few simple guidelines, it can count on congregational support: Do not expect money from the church budget. Do not plan projects that require help from members who do not share the same concern. Do not forget who you are in Christ.

New ministries have already sprung up. One group ministers to people recovering from alcohol and drug addiction. A second is for people with eating disorders. A third is for parents estranged from their adult children. A fourth is for victims of sexual abuse.

The new approach to service has brought fresh and surprising results. All four groups began as ways to meet needs in the congregation itself. But they soon opened up. Since they were meeting needs that members felt deeply, word got out. Friends told people with similar needs about the groups. So without setting out to evangelize, the groups have done so. Without targeting specific neighborhoods for service, the church has become more involved with the poor.

In the meantime, "the most wounded among us become our ministers and healers." In the past, many efforts to serve the neighborhood failed. Church members started from a position of power. They were middle-class Christians trying to help the powerless.

Now, however, church members are beginning from weakness that they share with others. Solidarity comes more naturally. Paternalism is less likely.

Of course, the congregation is not concerned only about itself, or even the local area. Four different couples work in mission and service programs in Central America. Recently a solidarity group formed to work for peace and justice in that troubled region.

One Sunday a month, one group shares a rice-and-beans lunch together. They share news of current events and how they are responding in faith to that news. Someone brings stationery. There is time set aside to write to government officials—and to pray.

The new ministries of the church are young and small. One has suffered setbacks and may not continue. But freedom to fail gives freedom to dream. And even small efforts are God's invitation to do more.

Listening, I was hopeful. I remembered the Samaritan's compassion. And these outward-looking clusters of Christians reminded me of Abraham. They are transforming the congregation. The whole congregation is freer to become an Abrahamic community that will help transform the larger community.

How Can We Join with Others?

Programs of voluntary service offer opportunities for some people to get started. We should only think of them as *one* way to serve. God calls all Christians to lives of service. God seeks to make the church a people who will serve the world through its very presence. If we confuse service programs with service itself we may forget this. We may think that volunteering for a few years or a few hours a week gives us the right to live as we please the rest of our lives.

But as long as we keep our larger vision for servanthood in view, voluntary service programs can play important roles. They train Christians for lifelong service vocations. They connect people of different cultures, classes, and continents. They allow us to live closely with people we might otherwise never meet. In turn, those people can teach us about service.

Ingrid Schultz has lived, worked, and worshiped in peasant communities in the South American country of Bolivia for seven years. A voluntary service program got her there. But her Bolivian neighbors have taught her that such programs are only one way to serve.

Ingrid is still amazed at the generosity of "people who do not have a lot of extra time." Women have laundry to do and wood to gather. Yet if a visitor comes by they always make a fruit drink. Men must walk great distances to their fields and work them by hand. But if neighbors are chopping the brush in their own yard, someone will always stop and help. Furthermore, as long as the whole community has discussed a school, well, or road project it can count on plenty of help.

The Bolivians have ways of serving that date back centuries. One of them is called the *minka*. When the time comes for a family to harvest its fields everyone else joins in. "The basic thing," Ingrid explains, "is that you provide the food and be ready to help when it is time for other people to harvest."

When a man in her church became ill at harvest-time, church members and others harvested his rice. "The church simply assumed that they would all get together and have a workday." This was always part of their culture. Now, as Christians, they have embraced it as the way they live and respond to each other.

Part of Ingrid's job was to coordinate the work of other foreign volunteers in the region where she lived. If a community wanted help from a volunteer it usually provided housing. Once, however, the development agency Ingrid worked with tried the North American way. Against her wishes, they paid a mason to build a house. It flopped—literally.

One problem was that paying for work created jealousies. But when the rainy season came, the house collapsed. The mason had only worked for his wage, not for the good of the community. He did a poor job. Now Ingrid had to talk to the community about rebuilding.

At a community meeting there was much complaining. Some wanted to know who would get the work (and wages) this time.

Then a man stood and asked, "What are we after here? Do we want to make money on this? Are we in the construction business? Or are we bringing the volunteers in to improve our community? Why don't we all get together on Saturday—everybody! Let's get these houses up, and let's do it our way."

The community would use its own building methods. And it would have a *minka.*

"Great idea!" Ingrid responded. "We are all going to come too, all the foreign volunteers in the region. And we'll bring the food along because when a *minka* is for a person, that is what they do."

It was a wonderful day. The women all came and cooked. The men mixed mud, cut down sticks, and hauled them with a cart and horses.

"I think the *minka* really bonded us to the community," Ingrid reflected. The new volunteers had lived there for a few months but not learned to know all their neighbors. Now they did.

"We had a lot of fun. There was a really good spirit of everybody working together."

Back in North America, Ingrid is trying to maintain the ways of generosity, cooperation, and service that she learned from Bolivians.

"They have been my teachers," she says. "The times I have chosen their way, I have been glad every time."

But Will It Really Make a Difference?[23]

An orphanage would not seem the place to begin moving a country from military dictatorship to democracy. Nor would fifteen people seem strong enough. But the Abrahamic strategy of social change works.

Often its power is unseen—like yeast in bread dough or a mustard seed starting to take root (Matt. 13:31-33). Sometimes its power is released through what looks like defeat—like on the cross. But there are times it breaks out for all to see. This happened in the early 1980s, in the South American nation of Uruguay.

Uruguay had a long tradition of democracy. Then in 1973 the military took over. It stopped twenty-eight magazines and newspapers. It censored those that remained. The police watched all citizens. They secretly gave everyone a code A, B, or C, depending on whether they thought a person might oppose their rule. Over the next ten years, they arrested one in fifty Uruguayans. They tortured many and 150 people vanished.

It was a culture of fear. No one talked openly. Organizing to work for change seemed out of the question. That was just what the military wanted. They could manage everything from the top. Meanwhile, the poor would not protest.

At La Huella, things were different. La Huella was a small community of orphans near the capital city. Father Luís Pérez Aguirre, a Catholic priest, had founded it for abandoned children. People treated each other differently here. The weak, not the strong, were important. Community members shared what they had. Young people learned to work with their hands and to think for themselves. They worked at what they did best, not what those at the top commanded.

Middle-class volunteers who came to help found their commitment to Christ and the poor deepening. Community members and volunteers committed themselves to work for justice in nonviolent ways. They discussed how to do this. In 1981 they decided to form a human rights group. They published a bulletin telling of the military's human rights violations.

It was a dangerous decision. No other human rights organization existed in Uruguay. Friends expected the government to wipe it out. For support and protection, the group joined a Latin American organization for nonviolent social change, the Peace and Justice Service (SERPAJ). In 1980 the international coordinator of SERPAJ had won the Nobel Peace Prize.

For years SERPAJ-Uruguay had only about fifteen members. Some, including Father Aguirre, were imprisoned. They were tortured. Yet their courage inspired other groups to form or resume activities.

SERPAJ started neighborhood soup kitchens for the poor. It worked with families the government had evicted from their homes. It urged labor unions and political parties to come back to life and work together for democracy. It helped family members find and defend imprisoned loved ones.

Meanwhile, international pressure on the military rulers grew. Evidence of human rights abuses surfaced. In 1982, the government agreed to negotiate with opposition groups. It said it wanted the country to return to democratic rule. But repression continued.

In June 1983, the authorities arrested and tortured a group of young people. For the first time family members signed their names to a letter of protest SERPAJ released. In turn, newspapers in Uruguay reported the families' accusations. That was a first, too.

The government reacted violently. It stopped negotiating with the opposition. It banned political activity.

SERPAJ members wondered what to do. Public protest was dangerous. Finally they planned a fast. Father Aguirre, another priest, and a Methodist minister would fast and pray for two weeks. For the final evening, they called their fellow citizens to join them in an hour of national reflection. They asked everyone to turn off their lights in silent protest during that hour.

SERPAJ had to depend on word of mouth. But word spread quickly. When one newspaper tried to tell of the fast, the government censored the article. So the newspaper came out with a half page missing. Everyone asked why. Word spread even faster.

When the fast began, hundreds of Uruguayans gathered twice each day for a silent vigil of support. To end the fast, the police surrounded the building where SERPAJ had its office. They cut off water and electricity. They arrested people in the vigils. But protesters kept coming to stand in silence.

At 7:00 p.m. on August 31, 1983, the capital city went black. It was the last evening of the fast. People had responded! The silence was eerie. Almost everyone was at home pondering three questions SERPAJ had asked. "What have I done for my country? What can I do now? What can I do for my fellow citizens?"

Then at 8:00 p.m., thunder. It came from darkened houses throughout the city. Everywhere people were banging on pots and pans. Driving around in frustration, the police had no idea what to do.

The tiny SERPAJ group and its fast had changed history. That did not mean they had changed the minds of the military rulers. Within a week the police raided their office and declared the group illegal.

But in the months that followed, a massive movement to end military rule emerged. Soon, 400,000 were in the streets. In 1984, the government re-opened negotiations with its opponents. In November, Uruguayans finally voted in national elections again.

SERPAJ members know that elections alone do not mean democracy. Uruguay, they say, must rebuild a culture of democracy and respect for human rights. They insist that human rights include employment, shelter, and health care, along with rights like freedom of speech and a fair legal system.

The group has continued to document the abuses of 1973 to 1985 so that citizens will never allow the country to return to military rule again. They have worked with a group of high school teachers to write plans of study that include education for human rights. They hold workshops in neighborhoods, hospitals, and union halls to help people find ways to include everyone in group decisions.

The role of SERPAJ has changed. Now it is the job of everyone to work for a just society where all take part and respect each other's rights. It has always been the job of everyone. But that is clearer now because a small, Abrahamic community took risks for everyone.

From Many Small Beginnings

God is calling us to discover a new kind of service. It is not the mixed-up service of paternalism. It is *jubilee*. It means sharing resources in just and biblical ways. It means empowering others. In this jubilee there will continue to be a role for compassionate Christians from the North who have technical skills and economic resources. But they have at least as much to learn from the churches of the South as they have to give.

The world itself needs a jubilee. Long ago Moses taught the children of Abraham, Isaac, and Jacob to call a jubilee every forty-nine years. It was a year for canceling debts and releasing slaves. It was the time to ensure that all had enough land to meet their needs. It was a time to share, and to remember to share always. (See Lev. 25 and Deut. 15.)

Things are changing quickly in our world. The superpowers of East and West are moving closer. Old enemies are putting aside differences. Old ideologies are running out of steam. Across borders once marked by high walls people are sharing new ideas, new hope.

But other things are not changing, unless for the worse. The gap between North and South remains. As wealthier countries of East and West move closer together, there is new risk. In their enthusiasm over positive changes in the North, leaders of wealthier nations may ignore poorer countries to the South. They may not like to be reminded that the numbers of poor and homeless people are growing even at home.

What would a modern, global jubilee look like? Can we really expect the "haves" of the world to relate to the "have-nots" less selfishly than they do now?

I don't know. But I never expected to see the Berlin Wall fall in my lifetime. And I have learned from the book of Jonah that even prophets of God dare never decide it is too late. God is full of surprises.

I do know that this jubilee must emerge from many small beginnings. Throughout history, empires have tried to impose their new world orders. Yet their power has never insured their success. Empires come and go, but Abrahamic communities spring up in every age and society. No one system will solve the problems of every society. Even world leaders will have to trust local people to find local solutions. Real change must begin among the Abrahamic minorities.

The people of Abraham, Isaiah, and Jesus are the original Abrahamic community. They have a special role to play. Throughout history the Spirit of God has pushed Christians to learn new ways of relating across borders, economic classes, ethnic groups, and races. Wherever the church welcomes this challenge from God, jubilee has begun, the kingdom of God is coming, and we can keep hoping for a whole new creation.

Questions to discuss

1. Are there "Abrahamic communities" outside the church and the Jewish community? How should Christians relate to them? Give examples.

2. Where and how might you and your Christian community begin to serve others? What can you learn from East Goshen Mennonite Church?

3. How can you join with other neighbors, groups, or movements as you serve? What can you learn from Ingrid Schultz and her Bolivian neighbors?

4. Does social change begin at the "top," with those who seem powerful? Or at the "bottom," with small local initiatives that seem insignificant? Explain.

5. Jubilee means sharing and redistributing resources. What do Christians from the North have to offer Christians from the South and vice versa?

Notes

Chapter 1

1. John Perkins, *A Quiet Revolution: The Christian Response to Human Need . . . A Strategy for Today* (Waco, Texas: Word Books, 1976) p. 62.

2. Ibid.

3. Ibid., p. 157.

4. Ibid., p. 194.

5. Ibid., p. 157.

6. Ibid., pp. 128-29.

7. Samuel Escobar, foreword to *Green Finger of God* by Maurice Sinclair (Exeter: The Paternoster Press, 1980), p. 3.

Chapter 3

1. Martin Luther King, Jr., "Beyond Vietnam" (address given at Riverside Church, New York City, April 4, 1967), in *Beyond Vietnam and Casualties of the War in Vietnam* (New York: Clergy and Laity Concerned, 1985) p. 15.

2. This section owes a heavy debt to Carlos H. Abesamis, *Where Are We Going: Heaven or New World?*, Theology Forum Series 1 (Manila, Philippines: Foundation Books, 1983) pp. 1-60.

3. The remainder of this chapter relies on Gerhard von Rad, *Genesis: A Commentary*, Revised Edition, Old Testament Library (Philadelphia: The Westminster Press, 1972) pp. 153-54; and Hans Walter Wolff, "The Kerygma of the Yahwist," pp. 145-46.

4. Translation is from Hans Walter Wolff, "The Kerygma of the Yahwist," pp. 137-38.

Chapter 4

1. Other references to Israel as God's chosen servant people appear in Isaiah 40-55. See 41:8ff.; 43:10-20; 44:1-2; 45:4; and 48:20. An important

passage related in spirit and theology is Isaiah 61-62 (compare 42:1, 4, 7 with 61:1-2).

2. Reinhold Niebuhr, *Moral Man and Immoral Society: A Study in Ethics and Politics*, with new preface by the author (New York: Charles Scribner's Sons, 1932; reprint edition, 1960), passim.

Chapter 5

1. Chinua Achebe, *Things Fall Apart* (New York: Fawcett Crest, 1959, 1969).

2. Ibid., p. 137.

3. Ibid., p. 135.

4. Ibid., p. 166.

5. Ibid., p. 162.

6. Lester R. Brown and Sandra Postel, "Thresholds of Change," in Lester R. Brown, et al., *State of the World 1987: A Worldwatch Institute Report on Progress Toward a Sustainable Society* (New York, London: W. W. Norton & Co., 1987) pp. 3-5.

Chapter 6

1. Hélder Câmara, "Un pacto digno de coronor vuestra marcha" [A covenant worthy to crown your march], message to the youth movement *Mani Tese* [Outstretched hands] climaxing a march on November 5, 1972, Plaza Michelangelo, Florence, Italy; in *Hélder Câmara: Proclamas a la Juventud* [Hélder Câmara: Proclamations to Youth], edited by Benedicto Tapia de Renedo, first volume of a trilogy, with introduction by editor, Serie PEDAL 64 (Salamanca: Ediciones Sígueme, 1976), p. 189.

2. For more on this approach see chapter 10 of my book, *And Who Is My Neighbor? Poverty, Privilege, and the Gospel of Christ* (Scottdale, Pa.: Herald Press, 1990).

3. The following section is based on Katherine Roberts, "Uruguay: Nonviolent Resistance and the Pedagogy of Human Rights," in *Relentless Persistence: Nonviolent Action in Latin America*, eds. Philip McManus and Gerald Schlabach (Philadelphia: New Society Publishers, 1991), chapter 6.

For Further Reading

Câmara, Hélder. *The Desert Is Fertile*. Maryknoll, N.Y.: Orbis Books, 1974.

Câmara, Hélder. *Hoping Against All Hope*. Maryknoll, N.Y.: Orbis Books, 1984.

Campolo, Anthony. *Ideas for Social Action: A Handbook on Mission and Service for Christian Young People*. Grand Rapids, Mich.: Zondervan, 1983.

Hall, Mary. *The Impossible Dream: The Spirituality of Dom Helder Camara*. Maryknoll, N.Y.: Orbis Books, 1979.

Kreider, Robert S. and Rachel Waltner Goossen. *Hungry, Thirsty, a Stranger: The MCC Experience*. Scottdale, Pa.: Herald Press, 1988.

Perkins, John. *With Justice for All*. Ventura, Calif.: Regal Books, 1982.

Schlabach, Gerald, W. *And Who Is My Neighbor? Poverty, Privilege, and the Gospel of Christ*. Scottdale: Herald Press, 1990.

Sine, Tom. *The Mustard Seed Conspiracy*. Waco, Tex.: Word Books, 1981.

Tillapaugh, Frank R. *Unleashing the Church: Getting People Out of the Fortress and into Ministry*. Ventura: Regal Books, 1982.

Glossary

Abrahamic community: A social group that has a visible identity as people who care about and serve others, including those outside their own group. Such groups are usually the ones who do most to bring justice and constructive change in society.

Compassion: Sensing the joy or suffering of others as though it were our own, and acting accordingly. Some Bible translations use the word *pity* where *compassion* would be more appropriate. But the two should not be confused. Pity is a mere feeling that may look down upon others without identifying with them.

Dissipation: When a community or social group starts to lose its distinct identity and becomes just like everyone else in society.

Exclusivism: When a community or social group refuses to welcome others to participate in the group, or is so different from others in society that others do not feel welcome.

Imperialism: When one group or nation uses political, cultural, military, or economic power to force its will on other people. Can be a form of paternalism. A form of *cultural* imperialism happens when we impose our solutions and our ways of solving problems on other people, even with good intentions.

Jubilee: A special time for redistributing resources such as land and releasing slaves or other oppressed people. See Leviticus 25 and Deuteronomy 15.

Mutual aid: Service within a community, usually to our own kind of people.

Paternalism: Treating others as children when helping them. This happens when we do something for others that they could do for themselves, or when we provide what we think is best for others without consulting them.

Samaritan's habit: The inclination to respond to other people's need.

Solidarity: Awareness of sharing a common situation as human beings.

Triumphalism: When one group, nation, or church is so sure its cause will triumph that it acts like it has nothing to learn from other people. It is the most common form of paternalism among religious people.

The Author

Gerald W. Schlabach worked as a writer and program administrator with Mennonite Central Committee (MCC), the relief and development arm of North American Mennonite churches, through most of the 1980s. Much of that time was spent in Central America.

He and his wife, Joetta Handrich, served as MCC representatives in Nicaragua for three years. While there, Gerald developed a regional "Peace Portfolio" for MCC. He later continued this assignment in Honduras. Gerald promoted theological education and practical training related to peace and justice issues with Central American church leaders. He has written various articles on the challenges Central America presents to historic peace churches in North America.

Since returning to North America Gerald has continued writing, been a homemaker, and resumed studies. He is the author of *And Who Is My Neighbor? Poverty, Privilege, and the Gospel of Christ* (Herald Press, 1990), and coeditor with Philip McManus of *Relentless*

Persistence: Nonviolent Action in Latin America (New Society Publishers, 1991).

He holds a degree in history and journalism from Goshen (Ind.) College, and a degree in theological studies from the Associated Mennonite Biblical Seminaries in Elkhart, Indiana. He is now a graduate student in theology and ethics at the University of Notre Dame.

Gerald and Joetta are members of the Kern Road Mennonite Church. They have two sons, Gabriel and Jacob.

PEACE AND JUSTICE SERIES

This series of books sets forth briefly and simply some important emphases of the Bible regarding war and peace and how to deal with conflict and injustice. The authors write from within the Anabaptist tradition. This includes viewing the Scriptures as a whole as the believing community discerns God's Word through the guidance of the Spirit.

Some of the titles reflect biblical, theological, or historical content. Other titles in the series show how these principles and insights are practical in daily life.

The books in this series are published in North America by:

Herald Press
616 Walnut Avenue
Scottdale, PA 15683
USA

Herald Press
490 Dutton Drive
Waterloo, ON N2L 6H7
CANADA

For overseas distribution or permission to translate, write to the Scottdale address listed.